Daniel

God's Man in a Secular Society

Discovery House
P U B L I S H E R S
BOX 3566 · GRAND RAPIDS, MI 49501

*PUBLISHING BOOKS THAT FEED
THE SOUL WITH THE WORD OF GOD.*

Daniel

God's Man in a Secular Society

DONALD K. CAMPBELL

Daniel: God's Man in a Secular Society
This edition copyright © 1988 by Donald K. Campbell
ISBN: 0-929239-05-9

Previously published by Victor Books under the title: *Daniel: Decoder of Dreams*. Study questions from *A Leader's Guide for Daniel: Decoder of Dreams* published by Victor Books © 1977. Used by permission.

Unless otherwise indicated, all Scripture quotations are from the King James Version. Scripture quotations marked NASB are from *The New American Standard Bible*, © 1960, 1962, 1963, 1968, 1971, 1972, 1973, The Lockman Foundation, La Habra, Calif. Scripture quotations marked NIV are from the *New International Version: New Testament*, © 1973, The New York Bible Society International.

Discovery House Publishers is affiliated with Radio Bible Class, Grand Rapids, Michigan

Printed in the United States of America
91 92 / CHG / 10 9 8 7 6 5 4 3 2

Affectionately dedicated
to Bea
loving wife
faithful mother
companion
in the study and teaching
of the Scriptures

Contents

Outline of the Book of Daniel

1

Have You Got What It Takes?

INTRODUCTION (1:1–2)

A prison chaplain noticed one of the prisoners sewing a covering on a bale of overalls. Greeting the man cheerfully, he said, "Good morning, friend! Sewing?"

"No, sir," replied the prisoner with a grim smile. "Reaping!"

As the Book of Daniel opens, the southern kingdom of Judah is about to reap a bitter harvest for long years of disobedience to God's Word. Judgment should not have come as any surprise, for as far back as Moses, the initial dynamic leader of the people, somber warnings had been clearly sounded (Lev. 27; Deut. 28) regarding the price of departure from God. The Lord had even given them a song (Deut. 32) that would be a witness against them in the day of apostasy. Songs are often remembered when sermons are forgotten!

When judgment came, it was for two clear reasons. First, the Mosaic Law specified that every seventh year the land was not to be farmed since it was a sabbatic year, a year of rest for the land, symbolizing that "the earth is the Lord's." But apparently the Israelites had not observed this law for 490 years, because the writer of Chronicles states that the captivity was 70 years in length "to fulfill the word of the Lord by the mouth of Jeremiah, until the land had enjoyed her Sabbaths; for as long as she lay desolate she kept Sabbath, to fulfill threescore and ten years" (2 Chron. 36:21).

Think of the patience of God lasting for nearly 500 years, a patience that had all but run out. For the northern kingdom of Israel, that divine patience was exhausted in 722 B.C. when the cruel Assyrians besieged Israel's capital, Samaria, and carried captive its leading citizens. More than 100 years later the cruel armies of Babylon came as God's instruments of judgment on Jerusalem. The lesson might well haunt modern-day society—God's patience has limits because He is also a God of justice and He must judge sin! An individual or a nation is foolish to imagine that God will never intervene to judge. The Bible and all of human history argue eloquently to the contrary.

God's judgment also fell on Judah for the gross sin of idolatry. Israel had been swallowed up by this evil practice in the forms of Jeroboam's calf worship and the worship of Baal. While Judah resisted it for a time, eventually the sordid story was repeated and there were even idolatrous orgies in Jerusalem. No wonder we read in Daniel 1:2: "And the Lord gave Jehoiakim king of Judah into [Nebuchadnezzar's] hand."

This was the first of three deportations of the Jews and took place in 605 B.C. The second came in 597 B.C. and the third with the destruction of Jerusalem in 586 B.C.

With this reference to the siege of Jerusalem in 605 B.C. (1:2), we are introduced to the great theme of the Book of Daniel, that is, the sovereignty of God in the affairs of nations.

We are taught here that God is the Master of the situation and that it was not really the superior might of Nebuchadnezzar that determined the outcome, but the good pleasure of God. Of course, He uses human instruments to accomplish His will—Nebuchadnezzar in this case—but God is always in control and the outcome is assured. No ruler is supreme, only God. No government can go beyond the limits God has established.

DANIEL IS CAPTURED (1:3–7)

If, as some suggest, Daniel was born during the time of Josiah's reforms (about 621 B.C.), then he was about sixteen years of age when Babylon's armies stormed through Judah and besieged Jerusalem. It was then that Daniel's world crumbled about him, for he and three of his friends were captured and deported to Babylon. Were they taken to serve as hostages to assure the cooperation of the royal family of Judah? Or did the king merely want young captives in his court to remind him of his great victories in the west? While these may both be partially true, the primary reason for the deportation seems to have been that Nebuchadnezzar was looking for choice young men who could in time occupy important positions in Babylon, particularly in the administration of Jewish affairs.

The requirements for selection were high (1:4) but Daniel, along with his three friends, met them. We learn that Daniel had no physical blemish and was pleasing in appearance. Mentally, he was intelligent, knowledgeable, and quick to learn. Socially, he was poised and able to live in the king's court without creating embarrassment for himself or others. Daniel was an unusual teen-ager, a fact that Ashpenaz was apparently quick to recognize. What a striking model Daniel and his friends are to today's young people!

Daniel and his friends had to be reeducated if they were to be of any value to Nebuchadnezzar. They were to be indoctrinated or brainwashed so that they would no longer think or act like Judeans, but like Babylonians.

Major Jerry Singleton was a prisoner of war in North Vietnam for seven years. Later, as a seminary student, he described in some detail how the North Vietnamese soldiers attempted to reeducate him and his fellow prisoners. Over a loudspeaker in their room came a constant barrage of propaganda, night and day, with the purpose of trying to change their political ideas. When I asked him how he was able to resist, he replied quietly but firmly that it was because he had Christian convictions and because the Lord strengthened him.

Daniel and his friends had a similar experience in that their captors bent every effort to brainwash these young men. For three years they were taught "the learning and tongue of the Chaldeans" (v. 4). Forced to learn the Babylonians' language, they then pored over Babylonian literature, reading the cuneiform impressions on clay tablets. They were exposed to Babylonian education at its very best, or rather at its pagan worst.

The goal was clear—change their way of thinking!

But this was not enough. These youths had been given names by godly parents that would remind them of the God they served.

Daniel, for example, means "God is my Judge"—a truth Daniel never escaped. Abruptly, those Hebrew names were changed and names assigned that would honor the gods of Babylon. Daniel's new name was Belteshazzar, probably meaning "Belti, protect the king." The new name of Daniel invoked a pagan deity, something Daniel could never do.

The goal again was clear—change their way of worship!

The tiny country of Albania has recently adopted ancient Babylon's practice by ruling that the names of its citizens must reflect that state's ambitions and priorities. *Christianity Today,* March 26, 1976, p. 27, reported: "[Albania] has joined the list of countries taking away one of the most personal and private possessions of its citizens: their names. . . . After all, someone named Abraham or Ruth or Mark might someday wonder where his name came from! And that could lead to a time-consuming search for a Bible or other religious literature. In the process, the unfortunately named Albanian might absorb some of the teachings of the outlawed book. That result, in the view of the government, would be very bad."

Still not satisfied that they had gone far enough, King Nebuchadnezzar even specified the menu of the young men (1:5). They were to have the same food and wine as was set before the king himself.

The goal is again unquestionably clear—change their way of living!

God's people today must be aware of the Enemy's brainwashing program. Satan would, if at all possible, change our patterns of living and thinking until we are conformed to this present age and culture. Not only do Christian young people in secular colleges and universities face this problem, but so do Christians of all age-groups because of, for example, the pervasive and powerful influence of the media— movies, television, and the press. Let us learn from Daniel how the Enemy can be defeated.

DANIEL IS FAITHFUL (1:8–16)

It has been said that while Daniel apparently did not object to his bondage in Babylon, to the learning of a new language, or to his other studies, what he did protest against in typical teen-age fashion was the food he was given to eat!

But his objection was not just a teen-age whim; it was based on sound convictions. The food set before him was from animals that were slaughtered ceremonially and offered to the Babylonian gods. In addition, the food no doubt often included meat the Mosaic Law declared unclean (Lev. 11). No wonder then that Daniel "purposed in his heart that he would not defile himself with the portion of the king's meat, nor with the wine which he drank" (Dan. 1:8).

Daniel could discern the fact that the Babylonian culture was in conflict with the Word of God, and he had the maturity and moral courage to say a firm no to cultural pressures. Involved in this is the clear implication that Daniel was a keen student of the Scriptures and that he had the ability to apply what he knew to the problems of his daily life.

How can we explain such discernment and moral courage in a teen-age youth? What were the influences in his life that matured him spiritually?

As a young boy, Daniel lived during the reign of King Josiah of Judah, that vigorous reformer who attempted to undo 57 shameless years of apostasy under his father and grandfather. The temple was repaired and the Book of the Law was found and read to the king and the people. As a result a national revival swept the land. Tragically, this revival had no effect on the sons of Josiah and when they succeeded to the throne they only sought to undo the righteous works of their father. There is every reason to believe, however, that the revival of Josiah's time had a deep and lasting effect upon a young boy named Daniel who determined to be faithful to God in all of his life

Daniel's faith and courage must also be a tribute to godly Jewish parents who had obeyed Moses' instructions to teach the Scriptures diligently to their children (Deut. 6:6–7). Daniel was given the most important thing to prepare him for life—a knowledge of God and a faith to live by in any environment in which he would find himself.

Daniel was a tribute to the worth of a godly family. A Japanese girl, while studying at an American college, spent a Christmas vacation at the home of a classmate. The experience was a delightful one, and when the visit was over and she was ready to return to the campus, the mother asked, "How do you like the way we Americans live?"

"Oh, I love it," she said. "You have a beautiful home and a wonderful family, but one thing puzzles me. I went with you to church and saw you worship your God there. But I have missed the God in your home. In Japan we have a god-shelf, and we worship our gods right there in the house. Do Americans not worship their God in their houses?" A thought-provoking and perhaps convicting question! If we don't worship God in our homes, we never prepare our families to live as effective Christians in our society.

But Daniel not only had convictions; he translated those convictions into consistent actions. First, he asked the chief of eunuchs to excuse him and his friends from eating the king's food (1:8). When Ashpenaz hesitated to grant the request for fear of his own life, Daniel did not drop the matter with a shrug of the shoulders. He next approached Melzar ("the steward") with the lesser proposition that they be given a temporary change of diet as a test (1:12). The special diet of vegetables would not include anything offered to idols. Daniel's faith was remarkable in that he believed that in only ten days God would bring about such improvement in their appearance as to convince the steward to change their diet permanently (1:13). And it came to pass! Daniel's faith was rewarded, for at the end of ten days the four young men had a healthier appearance than the others. Clearly, God had intervened to honor the faith of those young men who had put Him to the test. God, in fact, never fails the person who tries to do His will and who puts his trust in Him!

DANIEL IS REWARDED (1:17–21)

Is it possible to be well educated in our secular society and still believe in God? Must young people shelve their faith in order to advance in higher education?

The final paragraph of this chapter gives illuminating answers to those questions. The four young Hebrew men achieved "knowledge and skill" (1:17). The Bible states that this was a gift from God, though doubtlessly their intellectual prowess came also through the natural means of long hours of arduous study. In addition, and as a direct gift from God, Daniel was given special ability to interpret dreams and visions, an ability he would often utilize in the years that faced him.

At the end of three demanding years of study, the young captives from Jerusalem stood before Nebuchadnezzar for a final oral examination. They were tense moments.

The learned king examined them in Babylonian language and literature, found that they excelled in every area, and appointed them to important government positions. Subsequently, when Nebuchadnezzar had occasion to consult them, he found the Hebrew youths "ten times better than all the magicians and astrologers that were in all his realm" (1:20).

Beyond the fact that Daniel and his friends had excellent Babylonian tutors is the clear evidence that God had intervened once again to do something special in their lives (vv.

2, 9, 17). As the man of God had said to Eli many years before, "them that honor Me I will honor" (1 Sam. 2:30).

Daniel might well have prayed in the words of the psalmist: "Thou through Thy commandments hast made me wiser than mine enemies: for they are ever with me. I have more understanding than all my teachers; for Thy testimonies are my meditation. I understand more than the ancients, because I keep Thy precepts" (Ps. 119:98–100).

Of course, the Hebrew youths had an education that was unequalled, because in addition to completing with highest honors the "graduate program" in Babylon, they had received a thorough "undergraduate" education in the Scriptures in Jerusalem. They were able to "put it all together."

Modern universities have gone astray at this very point. Sir Walter Moberly, the British educator, observes, "If you want a bomb, the chemist's department will teach you how to make it; if you want a cathedral, the department of architecture will teach you how to build it; if you want a healthy body, the department of physiology and medicine will teach you how to tend it. But when you ask whether and why you should want bombs, or cathedrals, or healthy bodies, the university is dumb and silent. It can help and give guidance in all things subsidiary but not in the attainment of the one thing useful" (*The Crisis in the University* [London: S.C.M. Press, 1949], 52). In spiritual matters and in areas requiring moral judgment, only the Scriptures give us knowledge and discernment. Thus, Daniel was a student of the Scriptures as well as of his world, fully prepared for the difficult but highly strategic role he was to play all the rest of his natural life.

Little did the teen-age Daniel realize how crucial the choices were that he faced. How sad if he had adopted a philosophy of compromise and concession in order to "get along." God vindicated Daniel and honored him greatly because he stood by his convictions. God always does!

> Dare to be a Daniel,
> Dare to stand alone!
> Dare to have a purpose firm!
> Dare to make it known!

1—THINK IT OVER

The Book of Daniel is the key to all biblical prophecy. It is the foundation for a proper understanding of God's dealings with Israel and the nations—past, present, and future. As the book teaches eschatology (the doctrine of the end times), it stresses God's sovereignty over the nations (2:21; 4:17, 32, 35; 5:21). Great principles of prayer can be discovered in Daniel's devotional life (2:20–23; 9:4–19). The Book of Daniel reveals the blessings of obedience (1:8–21; 3:16–27; 6:10–23) and the divine judgment on pride (4:30–37; 5:17–23). The study of these great Christian truths can be of practical benefit to your own Christian life.

1. Begin by reading through the Book of Daniel and recording your observations in a notebook. List the major doctrines revealed and truths applicable to your daily life.

2. Read the text, observing chapter titles and subheadings, and give special attention to the outline (p. 8). You may want to record this outline in your Bible to help you grasp the major thought of each chapter.

3. Consult a Bible dictionary or handbook for background information that will enrich your study of the book. Read from a Bible dictionary about the city of Babylon to familiarize yourself with Daniel's surroundings.

4. Ask yourself the following questions: (1) Why was Israel in Babylon, exiled from the Promised Land? (Deut. 28:15–68; 2 Chron. 36; Dan. 9:4–14). (2) When did Daniel go to Babylon and who accompanied him? (Dan. 1:1–6). (3) Who wrote the Book of Daniel? (7:1, 15, 28; Matt. 24:15).

5. What principle is taught in 1:1–2?

6. What qualifications were required for those entering Nebuchadnezzar's training program?

7. What methods were used by Nebuchadnezzar to brainwash Daniel and his three friends? (1:4–6).

8. What creative alternative did Daniel suggest to avoid defiling himself with the king's food? (1:8–13).

9. What does the outcome of Daniel's proposal indicate? (1:9).

10. What does 1:17–20 teach about wisdom, knowledge, and intelligence?

The Babylonians sought to brainwash Daniel and his friends into their way of life by changing their thinking, worship, and way of living. How does Satan attempt to conform contemporary believers to the world? How should Christians respond?

2

He's Got the Whole World in His Hands

Two friends were discussing the dismal state of world affairs when one of them said with a shrug of the shoulders, "Well, why should we be so concerned? Things are going to get better. They always have before—and history certainly repeats itself."

Such a philosophy of history, held by many people, was also common in the ancient world, where it was believed that history was essentially without purpose and direction. The pagans believed that history repeated itself in endless cycles so that what took place in the past would occur again in the future. In essence this was fatalism.

The Bible reveals, on the other hand, that there is direction and purpose in history, that there is a personal God who is ordering the course of world affairs toward a glorious consummation. History is not an endless cycle of meaningless events; it is indeed "His story"!

In Daniel 2 we have perhaps the most comprehensive picture of world history found anywhere in the Bible, a panorama that stretches from Daniel's time, 600 years before

Christ, across the centuries to His Second Coming and the rise of His millennial kingdom. This sweeping revelation was given in the form of a prophetic dream to a heathen king, Nebuchadnezzar. It was in fact a "dream of destiny."

THE DREAM IS HIDDEN (2:1–13)

"Uneasy lies the head that wears a crown!" Nebuchadnezzar wore the crown as king over the great Babylonian Empire and at times he wore it with great uneasiness. One night, before he fell into a fitful sleep, he pondered his own future and the future of his kingdom: "As for thee, O king, thy thoughts came into thy mind upon thy bed, what should come to pass hereafter" (2:29). Nebuchadnezzar must have known that the kingdom of Assyria preceded that of Babylon. He brooded over the fact that the Babylonian kingdom and especially he, as its present ruler, could not last forever. What did the future hold? Writer Geoffrey King states, "As is so often the case, the cares of the day became also the cares of the night. Now Nebuchadnezzar did a thing which no believer in God should ever dream of doing: Nebuchadnezzar took his problems to bed with him" (*Daniel* [Grand Rapids: Eerdmans Publishing Company, 1966], 49).

On the other hand, we commend the king as a man who was concerned about the future. Too often men and women of today are concerned only about the present and turn a deaf ear to those who would remind them of a God in heaven to whom they must give account and of a prophetic Word that sheds light on what is to come.

Two men left the factory where they worked and approached a car belonging to one of them.

"What does that mean?" asked one man, pointing to a bumper sticker that read, "Maranatha!"

The owner of the car, a Christian, replied, "It means 'The Lord is coming!'"

"I don't believe that!" his companion snapped.

"Well," said the Christian, "I've got news for you. He's not coming for you!"

That blunt reply awakened the man to a sense of responsibility and concern regarding the future and his preparation for it.

God responded to Nebuchadnezzar's concern for the future by giving him a dream—a dream that left him agitated, troubled, and filled with a sense of foreboding. Sleep now became impossible; the king tossed and turned on his bed for the rest of the night as he pondered the meaning of the vision (2:1).

No doubt it was in the early hours of the morning when he called for his counselors, his wise men, to come and interpret the dream (2:2). These were the "king's men," his special advisers who were always on call for counsel. They fell into four groups: (1) the magicians (sacred writers or scholars), (2) the astrologers (enchanters or sacred priests), (3) the sorcerers (those who used herbs, charms, and potions in the practice of witchcraft), and (4) the Chaldeans (not used here in an ethnic sense but referring to a special group of priests or wise men). The fact that Daniel and his friends were not included in this group is probable evidence that this whole incident took place while Daniel was still in training. (See "in the second year," 2:1.)

The most highly educated men of their day, with a reputed ability to contact deity, were faced with a challenging assignment—to tell Nebuchadnezzar the meaning of his dream (2:3).

An intricate dialogue began between the king and the wise men. The king spoke three times (vv. 3, 5, 8), and the counselors replied in turn (vv. 4, 7, 10). The reason for the discussion is clear: The king asked for an interpretation of his prophetic dream, and the advisers were more than willing to comply. The interpretation of royal dreams was an art in which they were skilled. They even had manuals that listed various symbols that appeared in dreams, along with their probable meanings. There was just one problem— they had to know what the dream was!

But Nebuchadnezzar had no intention of complying with this seemingly reasonable request. The Authorized (King James) Version suggests that the king had forgotten the dream (2:5), but more recent translators prefer the rendering "The order from me is certain, that if you do not tell me the dream and its interpretation. . . ." Nebuchadnezzar, therefore, chose to withhold the contents of the dream from the wise men. How else could the king test the accuracy of their interpretation? If they could reveal the contents of the dream, he would then trust their description of its meaning.

The tension heightened as the king grew increasingly angry with the delaying tactics of the advisers. They in turn became more frightened in the face of the king's preposterous command. They felt the noose tightening around their necks. Finally, in desperation, they confessed their total inability to do what the king asked, asserting that no one else could do it either (2:10–11). They even claimed that only deity could reveal such things and confessed that they had no contact with the gods (2:11).

The king had the last word and it was terrifying! Consumed with anger, he ordered a mass execution of all the wise men in the kingdom including the trainees, Daniel and his friends (2:13).

The abject confession of the "wise men" is striking and set the stage for Daniel who is "a man upon the earth to tell the king's matter," a man in touch with the true God in heaven who will reveal the dream and its interpretation to His servant.

But the humiliation of the king's advisers is also the humiliation of human wisdom. Dr. Joseph A. Seiss rightly observes that the failure of the wise men shows "the incompetence of all mere human resources, learning and power to ascertain the mind and will of God apart from His own revelations." In an astute survey of the history of human thought, Seiss asserts, "Here was a full grown heathenism of more than a thousand years. Here were the combined strength and wisdom of the most noted schools in the highest acme of their glory. . . . If these men failed, it was the laying prostrate of all the wisdom, power, and art of man. . . . It proves to me, in one brief utterance, that all the religions, arts, sciences, philosophies, attainments, and powers of man, apart from God's inspired prophets and all-glorious Christ, are but emptiness and vanity as regards any true and adequate knowledge of the purposes and will of Jehovah or of the destinies of man. . . . It is to the modest Daniels and to the humble Nazarenes, after all, that the proud world must come to find out His mind and purposes" (*Voices from Babylon* [Philadelphia: Porter and Coates, 1879], 47–49).

The chairman of the Department of Religious Education in an eastern university acknowledges that there is "real concern in this country with spiritual and religious matters." Yet this professor, an ordained Protestant minister with a doctorate in Religion and Ethics from Columbia University, states, "The big questions have no absolute answers, yet they continue to haunt us: What is man? What is his relationship to fellowmen? What is his relationship with God?" But there *are* absolute answers because God has revealed them. If men persist in rejecting God's revelation, they have only themselves to blame if they continue in uncertainty and confusion.

THE DREAM IS REVEALED (2:14–30)

The Bible teaches that there are at least two great presuppositions or assumed truths: (1) God exists, and (2) God reveals Himself to man. These two truths appear in the Book of Hebrews: "God, who at sundry times and in divers manners spake in time past unto the fathers by the prophets, hath in these last days spoken unto us by His Son" (Heb. 1:1–2). And they appear again: "But without faith it is impossible to please Him: for he that cometh to God must believe that He is, and that He is a rewarder of them that diligently seek Him" (11:6). In Daniel 2, the same truths are illustrated when God intervened to reveal Himself by unveiling for Daniel the prophetic dream of Nebuchadnezzar and its meaning.

It has been said that the true character of a person is revealed in a time of crisis. Daniel faced a great crisis when the royal executioner stood at his door to carry out the decree of the king! The response of Daniel is an example of how God's children in any time should react to crisis. In addition, he is clearly shown to be a man of sterling character who has learned how to trust God.

What are the admirable qualities Daniel displayed? First, he showed wisdom and discretion (2:14–15). When under such conditions he might have said unwise and inappropriate things, he had the grace to guard his speech and inquire discreetly as to why the king's decree was so harsh.

Second, he demonstrated great boldness and faith (2:16). He was able to persuade Arioch, captain of the king's guard, to get him an audience with the king during which Daniel asked for a delay in execution and promised in time to tell the king what be wanted to know—the dream and its mean-ing. What audacity or what faith! Which is it? If Daniel failed to produce what he promised, who can imagine his fate?

Sir Wilfred Grenfell also demonstrated a robust faith in a time of crisis. In the course of his work as a medical mis-sionary in Labrador, he set out on a sick call with his dog team. Traveling over the frozen water of an ocean bay, he found himself isolated with his team on an island of ice that was drifting out to sea. Mercifully putting his dogs to death, he made a coat for himself out of the hides, hoisted a dis-tress flag—and then lay down and slept! After he was res-cued, someone asked him how he could sleep under such frightening conditions. He answered, "There was nothing to fear. I had done all I could. Certainly I had done all that was *humanly* possible. The rest lay in God's hands. What, then, was there to be afraid of?" (*They Met at Philippi* [New York: Oxford University Press, 1958], 155ff).

Third, Daniel and his friends prayed (2:17–19). "The rest lay in God's hands"—but would God honor the faith of these young men? The picture is a stirring one—four young men united in earnest prayer that God would be merciful and spare their lives. The result is not unexpected because "the effectual fervent prayer of a righteous man availeth much" (James 5:16). It would appear that after the time of prayer the four young men, like Grenfell, went to bed and slept. During the night, in a vision, God revealed the dream and its meaning to Daniel. Something of the thrill Daniel experienced in receiving this revelation from the God of heaven may be sensed in his immediate response.

Fourth, Daniel praised God (2:19–23). Instead of rush-ing impulsively to the king, Daniel paused to worship God. Praise is always in order when prayer is answered and in this expression of praise, called "Daniel's psalm," God is the object of praise. Against the background of the tremendous revelation received, Daniel uttered a sevenfold ascription of praise to God. God is to be praised because:

1. "Wisdom and might are His." God alone, and not the wise men of Babylon and their false gods, has the wisdom to order the world and the might or power to carry out His purposes.

2. "He changeth the times and the seasons." God controls the seasons or events of history, either in an active or permissive manner.

3. "He removeth kings and setteth up kings." In this way, among others, God orders history—by removing and setting up human rulers. The dream of Nebuchadnezzar that God revealed to Daniel graphically illustrates this truth, with kings and empires described as rising and falling in succession.

4. "He giveth wisdom unto the wise, and knowledge to them that know understanding." God alone is the source of all wisdom, a truth underscored for Daniel in his own experience.

5. "He revealeth the deep and secret things." If man is to know anything about that which is normally hidden from him, namely, the future, it will only be by revelation: "Then was the secret *revealed* unto Daniel in a night vision" (2:19).

6. "He knoweth what is in the darkness." God alone knows the darkness of men's hearts and the future, which is dark and unknown to man.

7. "The light dwelleth with Him." Though the Babylonian gods were considered gods of light, it is clear that light to reveal the deep, dark, hidden and secret things dwells (literally, "is at home") only with the God of heaven.

Having concluded his magnificent prayer, Daniel showed concern for the condemned wise men and asked that their lives be spared (2:24). Leon Wood comments, "He was not so occupied with his own importance (even though he had just received knowledge concerning the dream) that he did not think of others" (*A Commentary on Daniel* [Grand Rapids: Zondervan Publishing House, 1973], 62).

Then, ushered before Nebuchadnezzar by Arioch, Daniel heard the eager question of the king: "Art thou able to make known unto me the dream which I have seen and the interpretation thereof?" (2:26). Daniel's reply stressed three facts: (1) Reviewing all of the various classes of wise men, he insisted that no wise man of any sort could reveal the king's secret (2:27). (2) Setting God over human importance, Daniel affirmed that the revelation he was about to declare had its full source in Him. With great courage Daniel testified to his faith in God and gave all honor and glory to Him (2:28). (3) Disclaiming any credit or glory for his knowledge of the dream, he gave all glory to God (2:30).

Daniel serves as a vivid illustration of Peter's exhortation, "Be clothed with humility" (1 Peter 5:5). Sometimes Christians face a problem in this area.

Dr. H. A. Ironside, famed pastor and Bible teacher, was once convicted about his lack of humility. A friend recommended, as a remedy, that he march through the streets of Chicago wearing a sandwich board, shouting the Scripture verses inscribed on the board for all to hear. Dr. Ironside agreed to this challenging venture and when he returned to his study and removed the board, he said, "I'll bet there's not another man in town who would do that!"

Before divulging the contents of the dream and its interpretation, Daniel informed the king that it was given by God in answer to his concern about the future and that the dream dealt particularly with "what shall be in the latter days" (2:28). The expression "latter days" arrests our

attention because Daniel declares that it defines the scope
of the prophecy about to be unfolded. Found some fourteen
times in the Old Testament, it seems to mean an extended
period of time that is consummated in the messianic age.
Specifically, in this passage the "latter days" must include
all of the period covered by Nebuchadnezzar's prophetic
dream, namely the period from 600 B.C. to the inauguration
of Christ's millennial kingdom.

Because the Bible is a supernatural book, it can, and
does, have a great deal to say about the future. And this
should give comfort and security to the believer in contrast
to the unbeliever who "bites his nails" and wonders how
things will turn out.

Two men were listening to a delayed broadcast of their
school's crucial basketball game against a rival university.
Suddenly one of them said, "Why am I so nervous? I know
how it comes out." To which his friend replied, "Now you
know how God must feel when we fret and get so depressed."
After all, He knows how it comes out!

THE DREAM IS INTERPRETED (2:31–49)

With great skill and economy of words, Daniel described
the prophetic dream. The king was entranced, affirming
with a nod of the head that Daniel was on the right track. In
the king's dream, Daniel stated, he saw a great image or
mighty statue (2:31). It was frightening because it was so
overwhelming and the king seemed dwarfed as he stood
before it. Further, it was dazzling because of its metal-
lic construction—and the king trembled again as Daniel's
description renewed the nightmarish experience!

Daniel quickly described the four parts of the statue: (1)
the head was of fine gold, (2) the breast (chest) and arms
were of silver, (3) the belly (abdomen) and thighs (sides)

were of brass (bronze), (4) the legs were of iron, with feet
part of iron and part of clay (2:32–33).

At first the figure was stationary. There was no action.
Suddenly there was dramatic movement! A stone, super-
naturally cut from a mountain, seemed to catapult through
the air like a missile, striking the statue with incredible
force, crushing and demolishing it so that all traces of it
disappeared. Then, as the vision began with the great statue
filling the stage, it closed with the great stone filling the
whole earth. "There is not a superfluous word in Daniel's
entire description and account. It is a masterpiece of pithy
word painting" (H. C. Leupold, *Exposition of Daniel*
[Columbus, Ohio: the Wartburg Press, 1949], 110–11).

In subdued but firm tones, Daniel declared, "This is the
dream; and we will tell the interpretation thereof before the
king" (2:36). Daniel did not ask with uncertainty and hesitation in his voice, "King Nebuchadnezzar, sir, did I tell the
right dream? Was my description accurate?" Rather, his
voice rang with the conviction of a man who had been in
touch with God, had heard the Word of God, and, therefore, spoke with authority!

In the early days of Dr. Billy Graham's evangelistic ministry, he held a series of meetings in the Dallas Cotton
Bowl. As the services came to a climax, the challenge was
issued to fill the 70,000 seat stadium for a final Sunday
evening service. The word was out that certain gambling
elements were betting it couldn't be done, but on the last
night a cheer went up from the crowd as the last seat was
taken. A well-known columnist for the *Dallas Morning News*
devoted an entire column the next week to the event. He
posed the question, "How can a young man without a seminary education draw such a crowd of people when some of
the highly educated and robed downtown ministers preach

to half-filled churches on Sunday mornings?" Answering his own question, the columnist said, "It's because Billy Graham preaches what the Bible says. He has a note of authority in his message—a 'thus saith the Lord.'" And so did Daniel.

At long last Nebuchadnezzar heard—and so do we—the interpretation of the dream. In summary, Daniel stated that God had given dominion of the world to Gentile powers. Four such powers were to rise and govern the world. But in the latter time of the fourth power, the God of heaven would establish a kingdom that would crush all other earthly kingdoms and endure forever. The great kingdoms of history and prophecy are described:

1. "Thou art this head of gold" (2:38). Clearly the gold symbolized Nebuchadnezzar who in turn represented his empire. Appropriately, Babylon was referred to as the golden city because gold was used profusely to decorate its shrines, temples, and other public buildings. The Babylonian empire was grand and mighty and lasted from 612–539 B.C.

2. "And after thee shall arise another kingdom inferior to thee" (2:39). The chest and arms of silver represented the kingdom that was to succeed Babylon. Nebuchadnezzar wanted to know what would come to pass in the future (2:29) and he began to learn. His kingdom must someday fall and be followed by another. In 539 B.C., it happened. Darius the Mede conquered the city of Babylon (5:31) and Medo-Persia became supreme. Though a larger kingdom geographically, it was inferior in the quality of government.

3. "And another third kingdom of brass, which shall bear rule over all the earth" (2:39). The statue's abdomen and sides of bronze represented Greece, for it is made clear that Greece was the empire that was to defeat Persia (8:20–21).

Alexander the Great, who ordered that he be called "king of all the world," defeated the more powerful Persian armies in a brilliant series of battles and as a result his empire extended from Egypt and Europe to India. From 331 B.C. to 63 B.C. Alexander and his successors were indeed world rulers.

4. "And the fourth kingdom shall be strong as iron" (2:40). The iron legs of the statue represented a kingdom that was to arise to succeed Greece. That kingdom was Rome, which conquered all the lands surrounding the Mediterranean Sea and then took Palestine in 63 B.C. Luke's story of Jesus' birth opens with the words, "And it came to pass in those days, that there went out a decree from Caesar Augustus, that all the world should be taxed" (2:1). The mark of the fourth empire was strength, but it was destructive strength. The iron legions of Rome "crushed and demolished" all resistance. It is true that the world lived in peace—the *pax Romana*—but it was a peace enforced by the iron heel of Rome, a peace that stamped out freedom.

From a correlation of the Bible with ancient history, we can confidently affirm that the four kingdoms of the prophetic dream (vv. 37–40) have risen and fallen. Their ruins may he observed by archeologists and curious tourists, but as political entities they are no more. Rome, the fourth kingdom, was the last to fall in A.D. 476.

But what about the statue's feet and toes? According to the context, they, too, represented a form of the fourth kingdom, the Roman Empire, a form that has not yet appeared on the scene of history. And what about the stone that pulverizes the image and then fills the earth? How and when is that to be fulfilled?

It seems best to recognize that Daniel's prophecy passes over the present age and that this rather extended period of time belongs between verses 40 and 41. From our vantage point, verses 27–40 are history; verses 41–45 are prophecy. The prophetic dream reveals that the fourth empire, Rome, would appear and have a dramatic history, only to go into an eclipse till the end times, when it will reappear.

Mussolini said, "I believe in the resurrection of the [Roman] Empire!" But his abortive attempts to resurrect it met with colossal failure for he was ahead of his, or rather God's, time.

Note several things that will be true of the future revived Roman Empire: (1) It will be a federation of ten kings (see Dan. 7:24) that will no doubt be formed after believers have been taken to be with Christ (1 Thess. 4:13–17); (2) the revived Roman Empire will combine strong and weak kingdoms (Dan. 2:42); (3) it will have internal problems, especially before the rise of Antichrist (2:43; 7:24–25); (4) it will be in existence just prior to the return of Jesus Christ to establish His millennial kingdom, and (5) it will be destroyed by Jesus Christ at His Second Advent (2:45). He is the "stone cut out of the mountains" who will deliver a devastating and final blow against the nations before commencing His reign on earth. This passage is expanded in the Book of Revelation (19:11–21). There John declares, "And out of His mouth goeth a sharp sword, that with it He should smite the nations, and He shall rule them with a rod of iron" (v. 15).

One major question remains. Are there any developments on the current scene that point to the early fulfillment of these prophecies about a revived Roman Empire? If, as most Bible students agree, the coming of Jesus Christ is approaching, should we not be able to see some evidence of a grouping of nations in the geographic area once ruled by Rome? Significantly, we do.

With the decline of Britain and even the United States as world powers, western Europe no doubt will step into the gap. They will be forced to unite for economic and military reasons. It is startling to consider that an economic partnership of several European nations was formed in 1957, based on the Treaty of Rome! Today, twelve European nations hold membership in the European Economic Community, better known as the European Common Market. At a European summit meeting held in Rome in December 1975, it was agreed by seven of the nine nations then members to hold direct elections to the European Parliament in the spring of 1978. The nine unanimously agreed to issue uniform passports by the same date. Economic union is moving toward political union in western Europe! But is this necessarily to he linked with the prophesied revival of the Roman Empire? Here we must be careful because, though we now know certain elements of God's plan, we do not know when He will bring all this to pass. The Common Market may continue and be the preliminary form of a federated European government out of which Antichrist will spring—or it may pass away and be replaced by another similar organization. This much seems certain: Europe will become a significant power bloc in the years just prior to Jesus Christ's return to reign as King.

In conclusion, we are concerned about Nebuchadnezzar's response—and ours—to this great prophetic revelation. The king was all but overcome by Daniel's interpretation of his dream, and sensing that this was the revelation he sought (2:29), bestowed great honors on the young Jewish captive standing before him (2:46–48). But Daniel did not forget his friends and asked that they too share in his honors (2:49). Daniel came into a place of great power in Babylon, a place in which he could later play a vital role in the history of his own generation. It would have been too bad if Daniel had compromised when he first arrived in the court (Dan. 1). The fact that he didn't gives a strong clue to the subsequent success of his career. He was the kind of man God uses.

This chapter, so basic to an understanding of all God's dealing in history and prophecy, reveals three important truths:

1. God, not man, is sovereign in world affairs. Yet God is rarely recognized and His guidance seldom sought in the counsels of government.

A European ruler of a previous generation heard a Bible teacher who was touring the Continent and speaking on prophetic themes. He invited him to his palace, examined his charts concerning the future, and then asked him, "Are you telling me that Christ is to come as King and all kingdoms are to be subject to Him?"

The Bible teacher replied, "Yes, that's exactly right!"

"But," said the sovereign, "that can't be. Why, it would interfere with all my plans!"

2. Our sovereign God has a plan for the world. Men construct their plans, and when few are carried out, they panic or speak fatalistically of the futility of it all.

A politician in Washington, D.C., during the height of the Watergate affair, said, "Things in this city are simply out of control!" But they weren't, because even if man loses his grip on things, God does not.

3. God is ordering history according to His plan. Certainly it is not possible for us to understand how every event of our day fits into God's plan, but we know that history is not drifting aimlessly on. Rather, God is ordering all things to the consummation that He has planned.

Let us never forget that what is true for the world at large is also true for us as individuals. The sovereign Lord has a plan for our lives—and there is no true satisfaction till we find it and fulfill it!

2—THINK IT OVER

Modern-day worshipers know little about praise as it was practiced in biblical times. In addition to some helpful principles of praise, this chapter lays the foundation for the study of biblical prophecy by considering the interpretation of Nebuchadnezzar's vision.

1. What does it mean to praise God? Look for scriptural examples in Daniel 2:19–23; 9:4. What is the significance of this particular episode of praise?

2. Describe the four parts of Daniel's vision (2:31–35).

3. What was the prophetic revelation of each of these parts as interpreted by Daniel (2:36–45)?

4. Where does our present era fit into Daniel's prophetic chronology?

5. Which portions of the vision have been fulfilled?

6. What was King Nebuchadnezzar's reaction to the interpretation of his vision?

7. What position was granted to Daniel that later affected the history of his generation, with implications for our own?

8. Note several characteristics of the revived Roman Empire. (See Dan. 7:24; 1 Thess. 4:13–17; Dan. 2:42–43; 7:24–25.)

9. What present world conditions or developments point to a possible early fulfillment of these prophecies?

10. If, as Daniel teaches, our sovereign God is ordering history according to His plan, how should this truth affect our present daily living, our future plans?

The first thing Daniel did upon learning the king's dream and its interpretation was to praise and glorify the "Revealer of Secrets!" God alone is sovereign. He knows the end from the beginning. If God is sovereign over history, He is certainly sovereign over our lives. We need to learn how to praise Him as Daniel did, acknowledging His Lordship . . . whatever the risk to life or reputation!

3

Bow or Burn!

A country preacher determined to use the stirring story of this chapter as an illustration in his Sunday sermon. To his dismay he found that he had difficulty remembering the names of the three Hebrew youths, so he wrote them on a card which he inserted in the inside pocket of his suit-coat. At the appropriate time in his message, he paused, "Now you remember the story of the three Hebrew children . . ." and pulling his coat open, he continued, "Hart, Shaffner & Marx!" Hebrew children, no doubt, but the wrong ones!

While the names may be forgotten easily, the incident described in this chapter cannot. In fact, it is one of the most familiar of Bible stories along with the narrative of Daniel's brief incarceration in the lions' den.

The central characters of the chapter are Shadrach, Meshach, and Abednego. Daniel is not included, and the three friends do not appear in the book after this event. In chapter 1 they are portrayed, with Daniel, as young men of strong convictions. That thought is developed as they, apart from Daniel, are subjected to similar pressures to compromise their convictions and conform to a pagan culture and religion. Their story is told with grand simplicity: They are tested, charged, arraigned, convicted, preserved, and honored.

THE YOUNG MEN TESTED (3:1–7)

"Nebuchadnezzar the king made an image of gold" (3:1). Questions crowd to mind: When? Where? Why did the king of Babylon undertake this unusual project?

The time of the event is not given, indicating that it is not crucial to an understanding of the story. The fact that it followed the time of the prophetic dream of chapter 2 and the subsequent elevation of Daniel and his friends is indicated in chapter 3. "There are certain Jews whom thou hast set over the affairs of the province of Babylon, Shadrach, Meshach, and Abednego" (v. 12). This fact, together with the general narrative, seems to indicate that little time elapsed between chapters 2 and 3.

The image was erected in the "plain of Dura, in the province of Babylon" (3:1). The word *Dura* is still common in the Mesopotamian region and simply means "walled place." Just six miles south of ancient Babylon is a place called by this name where archeologists have identified a large brick construction, 45 feet square and 20 feet high, as the base or pedestal for the image.

The dimensions of the image are impressive. It was 60 cubits (90 feet) high; the famed Colossus of Rhodes was 70 cubits high. The breadth of the image was six cubits (nine feet). While such proportions would yield a rather grotesque figure, that may well have been the original intent.

The fact that the image was made of gold, probably gold overlay, relates the incident to the vision of chapter 2 and explains the motivation for the erection of this image. As

Daniel reviewed the parts of the statue in the king's dream, Nebuchadnezzar was told that he was the head of gold; that is, that the great kingdom of Babylon in the person of its king was represented only by the golden head. Impressed at first with the magnitude and scope of what Daniel revealed, the king was content.

But as he thought about the inferior kingdoms that were to succeed his own, he reacted vigorously. One writer reconstructs the scene: "In the next 30 days, while the construction of the golden image was in progress, the evil spirit of pride and rebellion in the heart of Nebuchadnezzar seemed to grow apace. More and more obsessed did he become with the determination not only to exalt himself but even to deify himself. The image was to be at the same time an object of worship and a symbolical declaration of the perpetuity of the kingdom of Babylon and a denial of the word that had come from the Revealer of secrets that 'another kingdom shall arise after thee'" (James R. Graham, *The Prophet-Statesman* [Butler, Ind.: Higley, 1955], 78).

The time for the dedication of the image was set (3:2). Invitations in the form of royal summonses were sent to all the military, political, judicial, and financial officers of every province. Though there were religious connotations involved, the chief purpose of this gathering was a political one. The image represented Nebuchadnezzar's defiant claim to universal and abiding sovereignty over his greatly expanded empire. The officials of that empire would now be called on to demonstrate their absolute loyalty to the king by bowing to his image.

On the appointed day, all the Babylonian officials were gathered in the plain of Dura, among them Shadrach, Meshach, and Abednego. Hundreds, perhaps thousands, were milling about, nervously awaiting instruction and possibly shading their eyes to look up at the towering, dazzling image (3:3).

Finally, the herald spoke, delivering the edict of the king, which was to bow at the sound of the music, or burn. Shortly after, the royal orchestra began to play. The great multitude fell quickly on their faces (3:7). But there were three who did not bow, three who courageously remained standing. There may have been some about them who urgently cried, "Get down! Didn't you hear the music? Get down or you'll die!" But to Shadrach, Meshach, and Abednego, it was revolting to think of bowing to any graven image for any reason. They remained on their feet, three lonely figures among the great mass of compliant Babylonian officials. Their strong faith, their unwillingness to go along with the crowd regardless of the penalty, has been a challenge to the people of God from that day to this.

When the Communists invaded a Korean village, they found a young man with a vigorous Christian testimony who, regardless of their edicts to the contrary, continued to witness for Christ. Determining at last to make him a public example, the soldiers commanded the entire village to appear in the town square. A Communist soldier led the young Christian to the center of the crowd, put a pistol against his head, and shouted, "Denounce Jesus Christ and embrace Communism, or die!" The young man hesitated, looked around the gathered crowd, and saw some he had brought to faith in Christ. Then quickly he raised his gaze to heaven and cried, "I believe in Jesus Christ! I believe . . ." Crack! And he was dead, inspired by a courage and faith similar to that of Shadrach, Meshach, and Abednego.

THE YOUNG MEN CHARGED (3:8–12)

No time was lost in reporting to Nebuchadnezzar the Hebrew youths' disobedience of his decree. Perhaps motivated by a despicable jealousy, the Chaldeans "ate the pieces of the Jews"—a vivid idiom meaning to slander or denounce another.

What a terrible vice is jealousy or envy! It has been called "the jaundice of the soul," and has been responsible for many crimes—the murder of Abel, the mistreatment and selling of Joseph into slavery, the hatred and pursuit of David by Saul, and even the crucifixion of Jesus Christ. "For envy they had delivered Him" (Matt. 27:18). But envy only hurts the one who indulges in it. John Chrysostom, the great biblical expositor of early Antioch, said, "As a moth gnaws a garment, so does envy consume a man."

The envious Chaldeans vented their jealousy as they stood before the king. "There are certain Jews whom thou hast set over the affairs of the province of Babylon, Shadrach, Meshach, and Abednego" (3:12). It galled the Chaldeans that foreigners had been given such important positions, particularly since their own appointments had probably been to jobs of a lower rank!

Three charges were made against the Jews: (1) they showed no regard or respect for the king; (2) they did not serve the king's gods; and (3) they did not worship the king's image. The first charge was false but the others demonstrably true. All three were intended to arouse the king's anger and even to accomplish the downfall of these insubordinate Jews and their replacement by their accusers.

THE YOUNG MEN ARRAIGNED (3:13–18)

Enraged, the king issued immediate orders to his guards, "Find Shadrach, Meshach, and Abednego at once and bring them to me without delay!" The scene was probably still in the plain of Dura. The guards made their way through the crowd of officials, found the three Hebrew youths, and pushed them roughly along to stand before the enraged Nebuchadnezzar.

Where was Daniel at this time? Why was he not with his friends? Since the Scriptures are silent on the matter, no one can give a final answer to these questions. It is usually suggested either that Daniel was sick, that he was away from Babylon on a business trip, or that he was excused from such a "loyalty oath" because of his high position. Lest it be thought unfair that he be excused from this severe test of his faith while his friends were forced to endure, do not forget that the den of lions awaited Daniel! God does not test all of His children at the same time or in the same manner.

This truth was brought home to me in a forceful manner when the teen-age daughter of a close colleague was in a serious automobile accident that left her with severe injuries. I watched, prayed, and to a degree suffered along with my friend and his family during the long months of uncertainty and slow recovery. During those months I enjoyed the fellowship of my own daughter and wondered why I was so privileged while my friend was so gravely tested. God spoke to me from this chapter of Daniel and taught me the lesson that, while He does discipline all His children (Heb. 12:6), discipline or testing takes different forms and comes at different times in our Christian experience.

When Shadrach, Meshach, and Abednego faced the king, their lives were in his hands. He did not have them executed immediately because he wanted to hear firsthand of their behavior.

As Nebuchadnezzar spoke with the Jews, his mood changed. First, he registered an attitude of amazement and asked, "Is it true?" (3:14). He apparently found it difficult to believe that anyone for any reason would refuse to obey his command.

Then, in an attitude of conciliation, he offered the young men another chance (3:15). "We'll strike up the band again, and if you then bow before the image, we'll just forget your first misguided refusal and everything will be all right!"

But the king's anger rose as he contemplated the possibility that these young men might not even bow when given a second chance. Again he loudly threatened the fate of the fiery furnace and contemptuously added an impious and injudicious challenge to the Almighty, "And who is that God that shall deliver you out of my hands?" Nebuchadnezzar knew there was a God who could reveal secrets (Dan. 2), but he refused to believe that He could deliver Shadrach, Meshach, and Abednego from the fate that awaited them.

The answer of the three Jews was classic! They knew the commandment, "Thou shalt have no other gods before Me. Thou shalt not make unto thee any graven image. . . . Thou shalt not bow down thyself to them, nor serve them" (Exod. 20:3–5). And they knew that for them there could be no compromise but only direct obedience to the Word of God! They declared plainly, therefore, to Nebuchadnezzar that *their God* (see 3:17) was able to deliver them from any fiery furnace if that were His purpose, but if not, they would still never bow to the king's image nor worship the king's gods.

But wasn't there another way out? Wasn't there some slight compromise that the young men could adopt that would make everyone happy? Today's Christians are sometimes masters of the "art" of rationalizing away the clear commands of Scripture. The three Hebrew youths could have rationalized as follows:

1. "We are not required to forsake the worship of Jehovah forever."

2. "We are not required to become idolaters but only to bow once. We can do that quickly with mental reservation and then confess it! God will forgive us."

3. "If we bow, it will be under duress for, after all, the king is absolute and we would simply be following his orders. He would be responsible and God would forgive us!"

4. "We need to consider that Nebuchadnezzar has treated us well, educating us and appointing us to positions of honor. This act of obedience would show our appreciation even if it does strain our consciences a bit."

5. "Here we are in a strange land, a thousand miles from home. Didn't the Scriptures predict that those driven out of our homeland would serve strange gods? Perhaps that means, 'When in Babylon, do as the Babylonians do!'"

6. "And what about our ancestors? They set up idols in the temple in Jerusalem as well as erecting altars all over the land. It must be all right—because everybody's doing it!"

7. "If we bow to the image, our lives will be spared and we will continue to occupy our strategic positions in government and be able therefore to help our people when they need it. But if we refuse we'll be killed and our people will be without our valuable assistance. Doesn't the end justify the means?" (Adapted from Matthew Henry's *Commentary on the Whole Bible IV* [New York: Fleming H. Revell, n.d.], 1039).

There is not the slightest hint in the text that the three young men entertained any of these thoughts. The spiritual issues were too clear, and so without hesitation they declared three things to the king:

1. *Admission of guilt.* When they said, "We do not need to give you an answer concerning this" (3:16, NASB), they acknowledged that they had no defense to make in not bowing to the image and were guilty! Those who believe the saying, "Every man has his price!" should consider well the response of these men in this crisis when their lives were at stake. They could not be bought—for any price!

2. *Affirmation of faith in God's ability to deliver them* (3:17). It is not to be supposed that Shadrach, Meshach, and Abednego had received a special revelation promising deliverance but that as students of the Scriptures they knew well how God on many occasions had delivered His people. He was a God of deliverance, and with stout faith they affirmed that therefore it would be in keeping with His character and power to deliver them from the burning fiery furnace. He is able to deliver!

3. *Affirmation of submission to the will of God.* "God is able to deliver us *but if not,* that is, if it is not in His will and purpose to deliver us, we will still not worship the Babylonian gods or bow to the image." They recognized that God's will might not be pleasant for them—in fact it might involve terrible physical suffering and death—but they were willing to obey God's Word regardless. Their faith was like that of Job, who said, "Though He slay me, yet will I trust in Him" (13:15). And they firmly believed that somehow all things would "work together for good" (Rom. 8:28).

The late Dr. William Culbertson, president for many years of Moody Bible Institute in Chicago, wrote out of his own understanding of this chapter:

The names of Shadrach, Meshach, and Abednego are written large on a page of history in the Word of God. A solitary reference, you say? Well, there is nothing small about these three young men, the exemplars in a special way of faith in the life of the believer.

These men had great faith. Their accusers spoke to the king: "These men, O king, have not regarded thee: they serve not thy gods, nor worship the golden image which thou hast set up" (3:12). When everyone else bowed to the image at the appointed time, these men stood erect. They knew the announced penalty of death in the burning fiery furnace (v. 6). But they remained erect. They did not go along with the crowd. They had the courage of their convictions. What a scene to stir the imagination. The Lord surely prizes stark faith. They had great faith.

But there is more. Arraigned before the angry king (notice the words "rage and fury"), they were calm and respectful (vv. 13–17). The king used a word that they laid hold upon. Said the king: "And who is that God that shall deliver you out of my hands?" (v. 15). But the young men did not need time to answer. They immediately responded: "We have no need to answer thee in this matter. If it be so, our God whom we serve is able to deliver us" (vv. 16–17). It took courage for these men to remain standing when everyone else on the plain bowed. Surely no one doubts that it took more courage to face an oriental despot and speak out. It is one thing to stand among the common people; it is another to face the man who has the power of life and death. They now stood nearer the doom announced by the king—but they stood! In this instance it was good to stand in silence; but it was better to speak of one's confidence in God before the tyrant. They had greater faith.

There is a greater faith than we have spoken about. There is the greatest faith yet to be manifested. "God will . . . deliver us. . . . But if not . . . " (vv. 17–18). Here is a paralyzing possibility. "But if not"—suppose He chooses not to deliver, or He postpones His activity? What then?

We say, "God will work"—but if not? "God will heal"—but if not? "God will answer our prayer in the way we ask"—but if not? "God will deliver"—but if not?

These men did not flinch. Do you? Shadrach, Meshach, and Abednego said, "But if not . . . we will not serve thy gods, nor worship the golden image."

Beloved, some of us may have the boldness to stand before men and the courage to stand before kings, but what about this third step? May we suggest that there is a greater faith than the one that asserts God will work. It is a faith that whispers, "Not my will, but Thine be done." Too many of us have lost our sense of value here. It is not the man who arrogantly or boastfully proclaims that God must work in a certain way who has the most faith—that is easy to say. Suppose, for reasons known only to Him, God says no.

Hebrews 11 records that some women received their dead by resurrection (v. 35). In the same context it says others were tortured, stoned, and sawn asunder. James was slain; Peter was delivered (Acts 12). Sometimes God says no. Then to trust Him is greatest faith indeed. (William Culbertson, "Unflinching Faith," *Moody Monthly,* June, 1971).

THE YOUNG MEN SENTENCED (3:19–23)

Nebuchadnezzar, thoroughly infuriated over the defiance of the three Jews, lost his temper completely and dropped any idea of giving the men a second chance, foolishly ordering the furnace to be heated seven times hotter than usual. (A slower fire would have prolonged their agony!)

The furnace probably resembled a modern-day limekiln with an opening in the top for the flames and smoke and another opening at ground level for stoking the fire. The fuel was perhaps charcoal with oil added to increase the flames.

The king's command was quickly carried out, and the flames built rapidly while Nebuchadnezzar no doubt thought to himself, "Now what god will deliver them out of my hand?"

Sentence was passed—the three Jews would be thrown into the flames (3:20)! What a terrifying experience! Since God planned to deliver them anyway, why did He allow them to suffer the ordeal of being cast into the inferno? Ultimately, of course, it is not possible to understand all of God's dealings with His children, but there must have been things He wanted the Babylonians and the three youths to learn from the deliverance through the flames. At the very least, the young men would learn that God is faithful to His Word. He had declared through Isaiah, "When thou walkest through the fire, thou shalt not be burned; neither shall the flame kindle upon thee" (Isa. 43:2).

The sentence was carried out with dispatch. Still dressed in the fine clothes they wore to appear in the plain of Dura for the ceremony, the young men were bound by the bodyguards (as if they could run away!) and thrown into the furnace. Flames leaped out and burned the king's men to death.

Many Christians might have pondered this story only to conclude, "I would never be able to endure such a test." But the testimony of many believers is that God gives supernatural strength, courage, and grace at the time it is needed.

THE YOUNG MEN PRESERVED (3:24–27)

Brother Bill Harrod was a boilermaker before he was converted and became a preacher at age 39. A muscular 210-pounder in his prime, he was candid about what he called "the sins of my youth. Before God started gnawing at my heart, I went in a lot for whiskey-drinking, window-yelling, and beer-joint fighting." Then God intervened in his life and turned him around. Brother Bill worked his heart out for the bodies and souls of the poor folks of West Dallas. His sermons were delivered in colorful language, as on the occasion when he preached on Shadrach, Meshach, and Abednego. "This wicked old king took and th'owed those three little bench-legged Israelite boys into the fiery furnace. But God was with them boys and they stayed cool as cucumbers down there and grinned up at the wicked king like three mules eating cockleburs!"

Nebuchadnezzar had settled himself comfortably on a portable throne at a safe distance from the furnace but close enough to receive cruel satisfaction from the execution of the men who had defied his decree, who had placed their trust in a God other than the gods of Babylon. But the king did not see what he expected; rather, he was shocked to see not three men in the fire, but four; not bound prisoners, but free men; not individuals who were motionless and unconscious, but who were moving about in the fire; not men writhing in pain, but instead showing no symptom of any injury; and most startling, the appearance of the fourth not like the rest, but like "a son of the gods." (See 3:24–25 NASB.)

The fact that Nebuchadnezzar, a pagan, identified the fourth being as deity is remarkable, though it is extremely doubtful that he would have had the insight to understand that he was in the presence of the Son of God. Yet most Bible students do believe that this was a preincarnate appearance of Christ, who also appeared to Adam and Eve in the Garden of Eden, who walked with Enoch, who feasted with Abraham, who wrestled with Jacob, who spoke to Moses in the burning bush, who appeared to Joshua as Captain of the Lord's host, who spent the night with Daniel in the lions' den, and who came to be born in a stable. God manifest in the flesh!

The king admitted defeat. Approaching the door of the furnace, he shouted so as to be heard above the noise of the flames, and bade Shadrach, Meshach, and Abednego to come out. They obeyed, only to be surrounded by a considerable group of high government officials who not only were consumed with curiosity but who would serve as a reliable group of witnesses to confirm the miraculous deliverance. The king and his witnesses noted that the bodies of the three were not burned or harmed in any way, the hair of their heads was not even singed, the fine garments they had worn for the great assembly were not changed from their original condition, and incredibly, the smell of fire was not noticeable. They passed the smoke test! In fact, the only thing damaged in the fire had been the king's ropes by which the men had been bound!

THE YOUNG MEN HONORED (3:28–30)

In the face of such a stupendous miracle, Nebuchadnezzar made a remarkable statement in the presence of his dignitaries, acknowledging that the God of these three Hebrews had intervened to deliver them (3:28a). He commended the Jews for their total commitment to their God (3:28b) and issued a decree that nothing "erroneous" be said about the Judean God because "there is no other god who is able to deliver in this way" (3:29 NASB).

The king had learned a great deal since he voiced the contemptuous words, "And who is that God that shall deliver you out of my hands?" (3:15). Sadly, however, the king's decree was largely negative in character. It did not direct people to worship the God who had revealed Himself so vividly nor did it deny the existence of other gods. Clearly, Nebuchadnezzar was not yet ready to yield himself to Jehovah.

The final note of the chapter is a reassuring one. The young men who were uncertain as to the outcome of this test (3:17–18), but who were willing to leave the matter entirely in God's hands, were not only delivered but "caused to prosper in the province of Babylon."

What can we say about the purpose of this record within the Book of Daniel? Does it merely provide some historical insights into the characteristics of Nebuchadnezzar and his times? Surely it is meant to convey more than that. The chapter shows:

1. That the times of Gentile world power, seen in panorama in Daniel 2, will be characterized in part by the persecution but preservation and ultimate deliverance of Israel.

2. That believers can remain true to God even in times of severe trial. Moral and spiritual compromise are not necessary. The courageous and uncompromising stand of Shadrach, Meshach, and Abednego has been and continues to be an inspiration to the people of God when tempted to waver from the right.

Of similar spirit was Athanasius, early Bishop of Alexandria, who stoutly opposed the teaching of Arius, who declared that Christ was not the eternal Son of God but a subordinate being. Hounded through five exiles for his faith in the full deity of Jesus Christ, Athanasius was finally summoned before Emperor Theodosius, who demanded he cease his opposition to the teaching of Arius. Athanasius firmly refused, whereupon the emperor bitterly reproved him and sternly asked, "Do you not realize that all the world is against you?" Athanasius quickly answered, "Then I am against all the world!"

3. Though a believer cannot know whether God will preserve him from trouble or see him through it, he may confidently be assured that the Lord will not allow him to be tested beyond his endurance (1 Cor. 10:13). Furthermore, God has promised that in every situation He will be present

with His own. Shadrach, Meshach, and Abednego were delivered. Stephen was martyred (Acts 7:57–60). But in both cases they experienced the presence of the Lord—and that makes all the difference in the world.

3—THINK IT OVER

Are there some absolutes by which a person can test situations and circumstances in life, or is all truth relative, after all? This chapter helps us distinguish biblical from situational ethics, to discover biblical principles that govern conduct in areas for which there are no biblical absolutes, and to respond properly to testing by recognizing God's promises.

1. Read Daniel 3 from at least two translations. Note the situation confronting Daniel's friends, the accusation made against them, and their response to Nebuchadnezzar's demands.

2. What absolute of the Scriptures were Daniel's friends following? (See Exod. 20:3.)

3. What rationalizations (presently called situational ethics) might they have used to compromise their conduct?

4. What does their view of the outcome (deliverance or death) suggest?

5. To what "gods" might Christians in our modern society bow?

6. What biblical absolutes ought to guide Christian conduct? (See Exod. 20:3–17; John 13:34.)

7. Under what circumstances would God not deliver a Christian from a severe trial or test? (See Rom. 5:3–5; 1 Peter 1:7.)

8. According to God's own promises, what is the believer's confidence in time of trial? (See 1 Cor. 10:13; Heb. 13:5.)

9. What was the result of the young men's faith? (See Dan. 3:17–18.)

10. What significant statement did the king make that was to prepare his heart for his later conversion? (See Dan. 3:29.)

"Here is a paralyzing possibility. . . . We say, 'God will work'—but if not? 'God will heal'—but if not? 'God will answer our prayer in the way we ask'—but if not? 'God will deliver'—but if not? . . . There is a greater faith than the one that asserts God will work. It is a faith that whispers, 'Not my will, but Thine be done!'" Dare we live our lives with the same quiet courage as Daniel's friends?*

4

Pride Goes before a Fall

Who has not had an embarrassing or humiliating experience in life? But who among us is willing to talk about it or make it a matter of public record? King Nebuchadnezzar, in a highly unusual move, issued a general letter to all his vast kingdom describing what was no doubt the most embarrassing incident of his life.

It apparently happened near the end of his reign, at a time when his elaborate and extensive building program in the city of Babylon was completed (4:30). It appears as the climax of God's dealings with this heathen king.

A remarkable passage in the Book of Job seems to describe precisely how God worked with Nebuchadnezzar: "Indeed God speaks once, or twice, yet no one notices it. In a dream, a vision of the night, when sound sleep falls on man, while they slumber in their beds, then He opens the ears of men, and seals their instruction, that He may turn man aside from his conduct, and keep man from pride" (33:14–17 NASB).

Daniel 4 records God speaking for a second time in a dream to the king. The first dream was of the great statue

(Dan. 2). God also spoke to Nebuchadnezzar through the excellence of Daniel and his friends (Dan. 1) and through the deliverance of Shadrach, Meshach, and Abednego from the fiery furnace (Dan. 3). Though it seems evident that the king was momentarily impressed by so dramatic a deliverance, it is also clear that he reverted to his former pride, arrogance, and self-sufficiency. Chapter 4 records the culmination of Nebuchadnezzar's spiritual biography, with God using drastic means to bring this haughty king to the end of himself and to faith in the God of Israel. Note how Nebuchadnezzar responds.

THE INTRODUCTION (4:1–3)

The introduction is actually a conclusion! Chronologically, these opening words belong at the end of the chapter because they grow out of Nebuchadnezzar's experiences that are recorded in the following paragraphs. But the king was so overwhelmed by God's dealings with him that, humiliating though it was, he wanted the world to know about it. Perhaps he reasoned that there were many others who needed the same truth he had learned. He therefore issued a universal proclamation telling his story, the story no doubt of his own conversion to the worship of the true God of Israel. The first three verses of Daniel 4 contain the superscription of this edict or decree.

Nebuchadnezzar spoke first of God's great signs and wonders (4:2–3). While these may include the preceding events, that is, the entire scope of God's dealings with the king, they must primarily refer to the stupendous occurrences of this chapter—the king's humbling and restoration to sanity and the throne. Nebuchadnezzar then contrasted God's rule to his own. God's rule is eternal and constant, whereas Nebuchadnezzar's had been just the opposite!

How completely different this proclamation from the ones Nebuchadnezzar had made previously. It can only be explained by God's work in the life of this heathen monarch, bringing him to repentance and faith in Himself. It was clearly a miracle of God's grace—as is every conversion.

It was December 7, 1941, when Mitsuo Fuchida, a proud and militant Japanese commander, led the attack on Pearl Harbor. But his brilliant military career ended with the defeat of Japan and the close of the war. Returning to his home village near Osaka, he took up farming.

One day Fuchida was summoned to Tokyo to testify in the war crimes trials and was handed a pamphlet as he got off the train. He was intrigued by the title, "I Was a Prisoner of Japan." It was the story of Jacob De Shazer, the Doolittle raider who was converted to Christ in a Japanese prison camp while reading the Bible.

Fuchida's curiosity was aroused from reading of the incident, and he went to a bookstore and bought a Bible. When he went home he began reading it.

"Every night I read the Bible," he said. "I read while plowing the rice fields. One night I read that Jesus died and that He prayed, 'Father, forgive them, for they know not what they do.' I realized I was one of 'them' for whom Jesus prayed."

At the age of 47, on April 12, 1950, Fuchida received Christ as Savior and began a new life. Though later asked to consider heading Japan's air force as commander-in-chief, Fuchida turned down the invitation and spent the rest of his life traveling in Japan, the United States, and Canada, sharing what God had done in his life. Nebuchadnezzar's conversion was no less dramatic.

NEBUCHADNEZZAR'S DREAM HIDDEN (4:4–18)

At the start of his narrative, the king described his situation and stated that he was both "secure" and "prospering" (4:4). In both his private and official lives he was in control of everything, totally self-satisfied. Who would dare rise up against him?

Then God spoke—it is well to remember that God can deal with ungodly men, even those in high and secure places, when human resistance cannot reach them.

The dream came abruptly, unexpectedly (4:5), and it frightened the king because it seemed to be an evil omen; it seemed to portend an impending catastrophe.

Nebuchadnezzar, in what appears to be a reflex action, called together the brain trust he was accustomed to consulting for answers. But as in the case of the dream of the great image, answers from the wise men were not forthcoming (4:6–7).

It can only be concluded that these men were charlatans, blind leaders of the blind. They professed to have contact with deity, but in reality they did not, proving that the plans and purposes of God are not known by mere human wisdom, but only as God reveals them (1 Cor. 2:14–16).

Dietrich Bonhoeffer once delivered a stinging indictment against his American theological education that is reminiscent of Nebuchadnezzar's experience with his "teachers": "A theology is not to be found here. . . . They chatter till all is blue without any factual foundation or any criteria of thought becoming visible. . . . They intoxicate themselves with liberal and humanistic expressions, laugh at the fundamentalists, and basically they are not even a match for them. Often it goes through and through me when here in a lecture they dismiss Christ, and laugh outright when a word of Luther's is quoted on the forgiveness of sin." (Mary Bosanquet, *The Life and Death of Dietrich Bonhoeffer* [New York: Harper and Row, 1969], 83).

At last Daniel appeared (4:8). Perhaps he was late on purpose so that once again the incompetence of the wise men would be apparent to the king and the true interpretation of the dream would have an even greater impact.

Without any delay Nebuchadnezzar asked Daniel to interpret the prophetic dream that had unsettled and frightened him. This dream featured a great tree, as the previous dream had featured a great statue. Nebuchadnezzar saw the tree grow till it reached the heavens and was visible to the whole earth. It was a thing of great beauty and its fruit was abundant and tasty. Further, it gave protection to the beasts of the field and lodging to the birds of the air. What an impressive sight!

As the king gazed on the magnificent spectacle, abruptly and without warning there came a command for the destruction of this seemingly indestructible phenomenon. It is a sad thing to see a beautiful tree cut down and no doubt the prospect disturbed the king, who was known to be a lover of trees.

But orders came from heaven, brought by "an angelic watcher, a holy one" (4:13, NASB). This angelic being gave a specific charge to hew down the great tree, cut off its branches, strip off its leaves, scatter its fruit, drive away the beasts and birds! A picture of complete destruction—almost: The stump and its roots were not to be uprooted, giving hope that the tree would be revived.

As the angel delivered his somber message, he interpreted the dream in part, showing that the tree represented a person (4:15) whose mind would be like that of a beast for a time (4:16).

The concluding words of the angelic messenger were most significant. First, the king needed to understand that the dream was a divine revelation of an impending event and not just an idle and insignificant curiosity. Accordingly, the angel declared, "This sentence is by the decree of the *angelic* watchers, and the decision is a command of the holy ones" (4:17, NASB). Of course, what was to happen was a result of the "decree of the Most High" (4:24), but it came in response to the angels in heaven who pleaded against the person who in his great pride ignored and obscured the glory of God.

In the second place, the dream had a deep purpose: Nebuchadnezzar, and all people, had to learn "that the Most High ruleth in the kingdom of men, and giveth it to whomsoever He will, and setteth up over it the basest of men" (4:17). This is, in essence, a restatement of the great theme of the Book of Daniel: God is sovereign over the affairs of men and rules supremely in the world. He is the final authority, the highest judge. Further, He oversees the appointment of national rulers. "He removeth kings, and setteth up kings" (2:21). "For there is no power but of God; the powers that be are ordained of God" (Rom 13:1).

Mussolini defiantly asserted he worshiped "no god save my own sovereign will." Nebuchadnezzar likewise had no sense of his dependence on God and said, "Is not this great Babylon that I have built . . . by the might of *my* power, and for the honor of *my* majesty?" History, both ancient and modern, bears clear and eloquent witness to the fact that God has His ways of punishing such proud and arrogant rulers. God does indeed resist the proud but gives grace to the humble (James 4:6).

NEBUCHADNEZZAR'S DREAM EXPLAINED
(4:19–27)

Daniel was distressed, even stunned, by the severity of the impending judgment of the king and stood speechless before Nebuchadnezzar, dismayed that he should be the bearer of such evil tidings. But speak he must, and with the encouragement of the king, he courageously told all. Restating the description of the tree in great detail (4:20–21), the prophet declared what the king perhaps feared in his heart—the tree signified himself!

The eloquent Dr. Joseph Parker wrote, "There are some things we must speak abruptly, or we never shall speak them at all; they must, so to say, be forced out of us: . . . 'It is thou, O king'—a short sharp stroke. Who would [not] vacillate when he knew he was going to deliver sentence of death, worse than death, all deaths in one agonizing humiliation? Better it should be after the pattern of Daniel, clear, simple, prompt, resonant, put in the very smallest words, words that a child could understand and repeat, monosyllables that made the heavens black with unimaginable terror—'It is thou, O king.'" (*The People's Bible* XVI. [London: Hodder and Stoughton, 1897], 402).

The rest of the interpretation unfolded quickly. Like the tree in the dream, Nebuchadnezzar had achieved great prominence as the head of all peoples and dominions. Because he imagined that this came about through his own strength and ability, he had to be humbled. And he *would* be cut down. His position would be totally reversed in that he would lose his throne, his wealth, the respect of his subjects . . . even his sanity.

The interpretation became a pointed application as Daniel forthrightly predicted that as the king had reduced himself to the level of unthinking animals by ignoring his Maker, so he was now destined to dwell among them. The sentence was clear. The king would live *with* the animals: "They shall drive thee from men, and thy dwelling shall be with the beasts of the field" (4:25). He would live *as* the animals—"And they shall make thee to eat grass as oxen and they shall wet thee with the dew of heaven" (4:25).

The duration of the sentence for Nebuchadnezzar was also clear: "Till thou know that the Most High ruleth in the kingdom of men, and giveth it to whomsoever He will" (4:25). The discipline in the form of this strange exile would last till the king learned what God was teaching him. How long, we often ask, must we endure discipline from God's hand, the discipline under which we chafe? The answer is the same as it was for Nebuchadnezzar: it will last until we learn the lesson God is teaching us.

A woman visiting in Switzerland came to a sheepfold on one of her daily walks. Venturing in, she saw the shepherd seated on the ground with his flock around him. Nearby, on a pile of straw lay a single sheep that seemed to be suffering. Looking closely, the woman saw that its leg was broken. Her sympathy went out to the suffering animal and she asked the shepherd how it happened.

"I broke it myself," he said sadly, then explained. "Of all the sheep in my flock, this one was the most wayward. It would not obey my voice and would not follow when I was leading the flock. On more than one occasion, it wandered to the edge of a perilous cliff. And not only was it disobedient itself, but it was leading other sheep astray. Based on my experience with this kind of sheep, I knew I had no choice, so I broke its leg. The next day I took food and it tried to bite me. After letting it lie alone for a couple of days, I went back and it not only eagerly took the food but licked my hand and showed every sign of submission and affection.

"And now, let me say this. When this sheep is well, it will be the model of my entire flock. No sheep will hear my voice so quickly nor follow so closely. Instead of leading others away, it will be an example of devotion and obedience. In short, a complete change will come into the life of this wayward sheep. It will have learned obedience through its sufferings."

God would deal with Nebuchadnezzar in a similar way, but at the end of "seven times" (probably seven years), the sentence would be lifted. Nebuchadnezzar would then have learned that God is supreme and sovereign and that he, the king, was dependent upon Him for all of his life and achievements. Further, as the stump and its roots remained, so the king could anticipate not only the restoration of his sanity but also of his throne (4:26).

Daniel's final message to the king came straight from his heart (4:27). It was a word of spiritual counsel that the king turn from his sin and practice righteousness. As God spared Nineveh from judgment because of her repentance, so might He spare Nebuchadnezzar. Tragically, Daniel's words fell on deaf ears.

NEBUCHADNEZZAR'S DREAM FULFILLED (4:28–37)

With direct simplicity the biblical record reads, "All this came upon the king Nebuchadnezzar" (4:28). The dream had its dreaded fulfillment—but not immediately. God is longsuffering and He demonstrated this by delaying judgment for twelve months, apparently giving Nebuchadnezzar a chance to respond to Daniel's advice. But the dream and Daniel's warnings grew dimmer and faded from the king's mind as the months passed.

On a fateful day, one year after Daniel's appearance before him, the king descended from his throne and walked out on the spacious roof of his beautiful palace. With a perfect perspective from which to view the great city of Babylon, he surveyed his magnificent additions to that metropolis.

Humanly speaking, there was every reason why he should take pride in Babylon. Many ancient writers have given descriptive accounts of its size and splendor in the time of Nebuchadnezzar. The city was surrounded by a system of double walls (comparable to a six-lane highway!) that were 85 feet high (comparable to an eight-story building!). The top of the wall was, as a matter of fact, used as a roadway for chariots and served as an aerial highway for rapid troop movements. Eight gates, named after gods of Babylon, gave access to the city. The famed Ishtar Gate opened onto the Processional Way, an elaborately ornamented street leading to the temple of Marduk, one of fifty temples within the city.

The palace of Nebuchadnezzar also adorned the city and was proudly called by the king, "The Marvel of Mankind," "The Center of the Land," "The Shining Residence," and "The Dwelling of Majesty." It is supposed that within the palace area were the Hanging Gardens, considered by the Greeks to be one of the wonders of the ancient world. These gardens, of such height as to be seen outside the walls, were said to have been built by Nebuchadnezzar to gratify the desire of his wife Amytis to gaze upon green mountains like those of her native Media.

Finding satisfaction in a job well done is certainly legitimate, but Nebuchadnezzar's response to the beauty of Babylon was something else. The king spoke with a self-glorifying arrogance that practically amounted to a defiance of God when he said, "Is not this great Babylon, that I have built for the house of the kingdom by the might of my power, and for the honor of my majesty?" (4:30).

The long-delayed punishment fell in the wake of the king's boastful speech. The voice from heaven may well have interrupted what the king intended to be a longer soliloquy; he certainly could not miss the connection between his proud words and the message from God. This message was the dreaded confirmation of Daniel's warning of the year before that he would lose his throne and his reason and would live like a beast of the fields until he took his place as a servant of a higher Sovereign.

James Graham imagines it happened this way:

> In the twinkling of an eye, Nebuchadnezzar became a raving maniac. With wild shrieks he rushed from the room and down the staircase as the crown of gold toppled from his head. Across the tiled floor of the throne room he raced, tearing from his body his regal robes and scattering them as he went. Through the doors and down the corridors he ran bellowing like a wounded bull while the palace retainers stood by in consternation. By the time he issued from the great door of the palace he was very little encumbered with garments of any kind, only his tunic and short trousers remaining, and these he also discarded as he continued his mad flight down Palace Way. Nebuchadnezzar, the proud and dignified monarch of the greatest empire of ancient times was running down the street of his capital city, stripped, stark naked (*The Prophet-Statesman*, 110).

For seven long years the once-proud king lived on the level of a beast, in a state of virtual amnesia. His case was perhaps similar to the soldier in World War II who, at a boxing tournament on an army base, was led around the ring between matches in the hope that someone would recognize him. Repeatedly he stood and gazed out at the unresponsive crowd, until in frustration and despair, he cried, "Will no one tell me who I am?"

Tragically, Nebuchadnezzar thought he was an animal, specifically an ox, and so ate grass like an ox. Medically, he would be diagnosed as suffering from a form of mental derangement called zoanthropy.

R. K. Harrison reports that he observed a young man with this affliction in a British mental institution in 1946. He describes the man's behavior as follows:

> His daily routine consisted of wandering around the magnificent lawns with which the otherwise dingy hospital situation was graced, and it was his custom to pluck up and eat handfuls of the grass as he went along. . . . He never ate institutional food with the other inmates, and his only drink was water. . . . The writer was able to examine him cursorily, and the only physical abnormality noted consisted of a lengthening of the hair and a coarse, thickening condition of the fingernails. Without institutional care, the patient would have manifested precisely the same physical conditions as those mentioned in Daniel 4:33 (*Introduction to the Old Testament* [Grand Rapids: Eerdmans Publishing Company, 1969], 1116–17).

Since there was a dreary sameness about the seven years of the king's madness, the biblical account hastens on to their conclusion and to Nebuchadnezzar's restoration to sanity and to power.

The king himself described the three steps that led to his restoration (4:34). (1) He raised his eyes to heaven, rather than continuing to look downward to the earth as he had done these seven long years. (2) His understanding then returned, indicating that the upward look was a silent acknowledgment of the sovereignty of God, a token of his newfound sense of dependence and humility. (3) He used his restored reason to bless, praise, and honor the Most High.

We are not told of the king's perplexity and shock over his own physical appearance—fingernails incredibly long, palms calloused like the soles of his feet, a long unkempt beard, hair that reached down his back, and his body covered with the dirt of seven years. But it all came back to him—the stroll on the roof of his palace, his arrogance and pride as he viewed the beauty of Babylon, the voice of God like a thunderclap sentencing him to live as an animal till he could recognize, honor, and serve Him. It all seemed so remote and at the same time so real.

The king now knew that the Most High God was eternal and that He reigned forever, something he could not attribute to the Babylonian deities he previously worshiped. Furthermore, no man could hinder this God or even question His actions (4:35). What a remarkable thing for the king to say after his recent and terrible experience!

With the return of the king's sanity, there came in quick succession restoration to his throne and even an increase in power and majesty (4:35). This was the Lord's doing and Nebuchadnezzar knew it. Unhesitatingly he declared, "Now I Nebuchadnezzar praise, exalt, and honor the king of heaven, for all His works are true and His ways just"—and a postscript—"He is able to humble those who walk in pride" (4:37).

Again we have a chapter that speaks to our world:

1. God alone is sovereign and supreme in the affairs of even the most powerful men, and man's place before Him is always that of humility.

2. God hates pride and will deal with it. Pride led to the downfall of Lucifer, the highest of God's angels, and it will ultimately destroy the unsaved man.

The mother of one of the greatest New England college presidents addressed a friend who had joined a church: "Elizabeth, did you kneel down in church and call yourself a sinner?"

"Neither I nor any member of my family will ever do that!" the woman replied, and her pride was just the reason why this able woman, with all her Unitarian admiration of Christ the man, did not come to Him as Savior.

3. God's judgment on Nebuchadnezzar is a prophetic pattern of what will happen to all proud and arrogant world leaders, whether an ancient Pharaoh, Haman, or Nebuchadnezzar, or a modern Mussolini, Hitler, or Stalin. One day, as this chapter seems to foreshadow, all Gentile world powers will be humbled and brought into submission to God. Our world in its pride and sophistication does not acknowledge Him. But the time will come when every knee will bow and every tongue confess that "Jesus Christ is Lord, to the glory of God the Father" (Phil. 2:10–11).

4. There can be little doubt that the godly influence of Daniel and the prophet's daily prayers for the king were used in a significant way to bring about his conversion. What is the impact of our lives on those around us, both our peers and our superiors?

5. It is a good thing to tell others what God has done for us. "But," we too often say, "I can't speak in public and I even find it hard to witness on a person-to-person basis." Then write a letter! Nebuchadnezzar did—and so can we!

Some years ago a Christian man died, and the late Dr. Donald Grey Barnhouse had the funeral service in Philadelphia. The attendance was large and included many business executives who had been associates of the dead man. A year earlier the deceased had written a letter with the caption, "A Testimony from over the Edge of My Grave" and put it in his papers, asking that it be read at his funeral.

Dr. Barnhouse opened the letter and began to read: "This is my funeral service, but I want it to be a time of testimony. Mac, I suppose you're in the audience looking at my casket. My, how many times I've played golf with you to seek to bring the gospel to your heart and you wouldn't hear! George, why have you continued to reject Jesus Christ when He died for you and offers eternal life now?"

By this time, different persons in the audience were squirming, afraid they would be addressed next. We should not wait till we die, but should speak up for Christ now, or at least write a letter of testimony to a lost friend we've been praying for!

4—THINK IT OVER

Nebuchadnezzar's problem was his pride. Pride may be a virtue—self-respect, dignity, self-worth—but more often it is a vice—sinful arrogance and presumption. If this happens to be your weakness, take heed. This chapter emphasizes God's attitude toward pride and His none-too-gentle approach to dealing with it. As a Christian, you can avoid the painful consequences of a prideful spirit if you'll learn from Nebuchadnezzar's example.

1. Distinguish between proper and improper pride, using the following biblical references: Psalm 31:23, 94:2; Proverbs 21:4, 24; Mark 7:22–23; 1 John 2:16.

2. What is God's attitude toward pride? (See Prov. 6:16–17, 16:5; 1 Peter 5:5.)

3. How does pride affect our relationship with God? With other people? (See Ps. 10:4; Prov. 6:16–17; 13:10; 28:25; 1 Peter 5:5.)

4. How does God deal with pride? (See 1 Sam. 2:7; 2 Chron. 26:16–23; 32:24–26; Job 33:14–17; Prov. 11:2; 15:25; Dan. 4:30, 37; 5:20; Mal. 4:1; Luke 1:51.)

5. How should believers deal with pride? How can they avoid it? (See Prov. 8:13; 11:2; 16:19; 18:12; 29:23; Mark 10:35–45; John 13:1–17; Phil. 2:5–8; Rom. 12:1; 1 Peter 3:8; 5:6; 1 John 1:9; 2:15–16.)

6. How is pride related to the fall of man? To the fall of Satan? (See Gen. 3:1–7; Isa. 14:12–14; Ezek. 28:11–19; 1 Tim. 3:6.)

7. Trace Nebuchadnezzar's spiritual pilgrimage, referring to Daniel 2:47, 3:28–29, and 4:1–3; 34–37. What three agents were used in his "awakening"?

8. Which of these methods of evangelism might be used or adapted for use in reaching friends and associates with the gospel?

9. From Daniel 4, what spiritual truths are found in Nebuchadnezzar's testimony?

10. What poignant story about a Swiss shepherd (from the text) illustrates the lengths to which God will go to reach a wayward "sheep"?

Kind Shepherd, I am amazed by Your faithful love and care. When I was lost, You found me. When I foolishly stray from Your path, You do not rest until my course is corrected. With Your rod and staff, You guarantee my protection. You lead me beside still waters and into green pastures, and I know I shall dwell safely in Your fold forever!

5

The Bigger They Are, The Harder They Fall

A recent family trip included visits to Gettysburg, Washington, Williamsburg, and Jamestown—names that conjure up so many stirring stories of the colonial days and Civil War in the United States. In Washington we gazed at the original copies of the Constitution, Bill of Rights, and Declaration of Independence. Certainly, the founders of our nation were men of great courage and high resolve. But nations not only rise; they also fall. And Daniel 5 records the downfall of a great kingdom, a kingdom that thought itself eternal but was weighed in the balances and found wanting.

A clear warning is sounded by the events of this chapter and by the demise of other civilizations as well. In 1976, Americans celebrated the two hundredth anniversary of their nation's birth and passed by with scarcely a comment the fifteen hundredth anniversary of the death of Rome in A.D. 476. Some modern historians, students of both events, have pointed to a parallel decline of western civilization, and *Time* magazine, in a bicentennial essay, acknowledged that "the echoes of the Old World and this one are chilling" (August 23, 1976).

Daniel affirmed: "He [God] removeth kings and setteth up kings" (2:21). The prophet then interpreted the image vision, which showed how God would do this with a succession of kings and kingdoms—Babylon, Persia, Greece, and Rome. Significantly, Daniel 5 records the fulfillment of the first part of that vision with the fall of Babylon and the rise of Persia.

But this chapter is also significant for its demonstration of the trustworthiness of the Book of Daniel, and by extension, all of Scripture. One writer claimed that this chapter is "notable for its historic inconsistencies." Bible critics have stumbled over the words of the chapter, "Belshazzar the king," because the ancient historians cited Nabonidus as the last king of Babylon and made no mention of Belshazzar. Is the Book of Daniel in error on this point?

As a matter of fact, archeology has demonstrated that both the classical historians and the Bible are accurate. Babylonian cuneiform documents, such as the "Nabonidus Chronicle," confirm that Belshazzar was the eldest son and co-regent of Nabonidus, reigning in that capacity from 553–539 B.C. This explains the action of Belshazzar (5:29) in making Daniel a third ruler in the kingdom.

And this is only one point at which this chapter exhibits remarkable accuracy. When confronted with a supposed error in the Scriptures, therefore, the better part of wisdom is to withhold judgment until man's knowledge "catches up" with biblical statements. In every case the sacred record has been substantiated.

A NIGHT OF REVELRY (5:1–4)

The year was 539 B.C. The great city of Babylon faced a crisis of survival because the Persian armies had surrounded her massive walls and were trying to breach them. No doubt Belshazzar sensed the fright of his people and therefore staged a magnificent banquet to bolster their sagging morale and to show his own faith in Babylon's gods and strong fortifications.

It was a feast at which the wine flowed freely, the king setting an example before his lords and then before his wives and concubines (v. 2). The presence of women at such banquets was normally forbidden and probably indicates that moral restraints were released under the influence of alcohol.

James Graham recreates the scene:

As the banquet progressed, Belshazzar would leap to his feet and call upon the guests to join him in drinking toasts first to Bel, then to each one, in order, of the Babylonian idols that were placed around the walls. Every guest would rise and drink to the toast each time the king demanded it until men and women were all in an advanced stage of inebriation, with an increasing breakdown of all moral restraint that invariably accompanies such debauchery and idolatry. Brazen licentiousness was a part of the worship of Bel, and this wicked Bacchanalian orgy degenerated into indiscriminate promiscuity between men and women as they would retire to the adjoining apartments of the palace, and some were so intoxicated that they would shamelessly indulge their lusts even in the brilliant light of the banquet-hall itself. Small wonder that Belshazzar's notorious feast has come down in history as a symbol and synonym of unbridled drunkenness and lust and of the very acme of wickedness and debauchery (*The Prophet-Statesman,* 78).

Under the influence of alcohol Belshazzar made another and very costly mistake. He commanded that the sacred vessels, carried to Babylon by his ancestor Nebuchadnezzar nearly fifty years before, be brought into the banquet hall where they would be used as drinking cups. He intended to demonstrate the superiority of the Babylonian deities over the God of the Hebrews. Perhaps remembering Nebuchadnezzar's humiliating experience brought about by this God (Dan. 4), Belshazzar wanted to show he would not thus be intimidated and so perpetrated this bold act of defiance. It was plainly calculated to insult the God whose temple had stood in Jerusalem. And so "they drank wine, and praised the gods of gold, and of silver, of brass, of iron, of wood, and of stone" (v. 4)—and challenged the God whose vessels they were using to stop them if He could! God accepted the challenge!

A NIGHT OF REVELATION (5:5–29)

The night of revelry became a night of revelation. God interrupted the boisterous banquet with a message, warning of impending doom.

At the height of the celebration in the banquet hall of the palace, the fingers of a man's hand suddenly appeared and began to write on the plastered wall. The writing was large and vivid; no one could miss it. The effect was immediate as a deathly silence fell over the crowd and fear gripped the people.

The responses of Belshazzar, the queen mother, and the prophet Daniel to this decisive intervention of God are traced in sequence.

The response of Belshazzar. The king was completely befuddled and terrified. A deadly pallor crept over his face as he viewed the strange writing, the wine cup fell from his shaking hands and crashed to the floor, his mind was seized with fright, and he became weak all over. With a hollow voice he cried for his wise men to whom he offered great rewards if they could give the interpretation of the writing that remained visible on the wall. But they could not. Once again the "wise men" demonstrated their utter inability to understand the mind of God and His revealed Word. That privilege belongs to those who know Him!

The advice of the queen mother. While the entire crowd from king to lords, wives, concubines, and wise men stood perplexed and frightened, another person entered the banquet hall—the queen mother. It is thought that she was Nitocris, daughter of Nebuchadnezzar, wife of Nabonidus and mother of Belshazzar.

With a glance she surveyed the scene and then addressed her son the king. Her advice was twofold. First, she counseled him to "pull himself together" (v. 10). Next, she told him of Daniel and urged that he be called to explain the handwriting on the wall.

The queen mother, in describing Daniel's rare gifts, used the same phrases as had Nebuchadnezzar. (Compare 5:11–12 with 4:8–9, 18.) No doubt she had not only heard her father speak of Daniel in this way but had also witnessed firsthand the prophet's abilities to interpret dreams, solve riddles, and answer knotty problems.

The appearance of Daniel. Belshazzar was desperate. He was ready to listen to anyone who could help and quickly followed the counsel of the queen mother, summoning Daniel to appear. When he came, Belshazzar greeted him: "So you are Daniel, one of the captives my grandfather brought out of Judah! Why, I have heard of you! I understand that the Spirit of God is within you and that you are filled with enlightenment and wisdom" (vv. 13–14, author's paraphrase).

Profligate man that he was, Belshazzar had never taken the time to consult the prophet of God. Now he turned in desperation to the man he had long ignored.

Dr. Joseph Parker comments movingly on this event:

> Preachers of the Word, you will be wanted some day by Belshazzar; you were not at the beginning of the feast, but you will be there before the banqueting hall is closed; the king will not ask you to drink wine, but he will ask you to tell the secret of his pain and heal the malady of his heart. Abide your time. You are nobody now. . . . Midway down the programme to mention pulpit, or preacher, or Bible, would be to violate the harmony of the occasion. But the preacher, as we have often had occasion to say, will have his opportunity. They will send for him when all other friends have failed; may he then come fearlessly, independently, asking only to be made a medium through which divine communications can be addressed to the listening trouble of the world. . . . O Daniel, preacher, speaker, teacher, thunder out God's word, if it be a case of judgment and doom; or whisper it, or rain in gracious tears, if it be a message of sympathy and love and welcome (*The People's Bible*, 415–16).

As the king was speaking, the aged prophet observed the scene about him. The evidences of sin and degeneracy were clear and were an offense to the man who had walked with God all his life. No doubt his own stately bearing and dignified appearance brought a hush to the hall and cast a spell over the dissipated revelers.

For many years Daniel had prayed for an opportunity to speak of God to the king and now that opportunity was present. Daniel was over eighty years of age, but he was tall and straight in body and spirit as he looked into the eyes of the pale, trembling king and began to speak. He delivered a sermon intended primarily for the king, but surely heard by everyone in the room. And what a sermon it was! Not a sound was heard as the man of God first refused the king's gifts lest it be thought his message was influenced by them. He then proceeded to give Belshazzar a lesson from history, an excellent source of instruction (vv. 18–21). He reminded the king that God had given his grandfather Nebuchadnezzar a kingdom but that he was filled with pride and refused to acknowledge that he was indebted to God for all he possessed. Therefore, God humbled him and caused him to live like a beast of the field till he learned that Jehovah was sovereign and that he and all men were accountable to Him.

But Daniel did not leave it to Belshazzar to make the application to himself. The prophet indicted the king on three weighty charges. First, he charged him with sinning against the light of knowledge (v. 22). Belshazzar knew all about his grandfather Nebuchadnezzar's experience, but he did not learn from it. He did not profit in any way, did not heed the warning, did not learn from history and humble himself before God. As a sad result, judgment would fall very soon on this king and his kingdom.

God expects men to respond to the light He gives. When they do not, judgment is the only alternative. During Jesus' earthly ministry, He spent a great deal of time performing miracles and preaching sermons in and about the villages of Chorazin, Bethsaida, and Capernaum. In the main, the only response was a languid indifference and abject unbelief. Jesus announced, therefore, that they would receive greater judgment than the wicked cities of Tyre, Sidon, and Sodom—because they had received greater light!

God holds men responsible for the truth He reveals to them. To Belshazzar, only a comparatively small amount of truth was revealed, and he was held responsible. How much greater the responsibility and accountability of men today who are exposed to the Word of God by radio, television, the printed page, in churches, camps, conferences, and seminars—and yet do not believe!

The second charge against Belshazzar was that he deliberately defied God (v. 23). This was not the case of a man who sinned in ignorance. It was plainly the case of a man who willfully exalted himself against the Lord of heaven. Belshazzar demonstrated his defiance by purposely desecrating the sacred vessels, perhaps to attempt to show that he would not be intimidated by the God of the Hebrews as had his ancestor Nebuchadnezzar.

A similar defiant spirit is expressed in a poem written by the American poet, Sara Teasdale:

> I would not have a God come in
> To shield me suddenly from sin,
> And set my house of life to rights;
> Nor angels with bright burning wings
> Ordering my thoughts and things:
> Rather my own frail guttering lights
> Windblown and nearly beaten out,
> Rather the terror of the nights
> And long sick groping after doubt.
> Rather be lost than let my soul
> Slip vaguely from my own control—
> Of my own spirit let me be
> In sole, though feeble, mastery.
>   (Appeared in *Our Hope* magazine, November 1938).

The third charge against Belshazzar was that he worshiped idols (v. 23). Courageously, and with scorching sarcasm, Daniel accused the king of worshiping idols "which see not, nor hear, nor know." What a contrast between the God who had intervened in Nebuchadnezzar's life and who was speaking in this darkened banquet hall, and the deaf and dumb idols worshiped by the Babylonians!

As a consequence of worshiping false gods, the king did not acknowledge the true God. Daniel's words were piercing and meaningful. "And the God in whose hand thy breath is and . . . all thy ways, has thou not glorified" (v. 23). Belshazzar surely did not realize that his very breath came from the hand of God. He did not know that all his ways were under God's supervision. He did not comprehend that his purpose in life was to glorify God. Instead, he imagined that he was master of his own fate and captain of his own soul.

So wrote William Henley in his poem, "Invictus":

> Out of the night that covers me,
> Black as the pit from pole to pole,
> I thank whatever gods may be,
> For my unconquerable soul.
>
> In the fell clutch of circumstance
> I have not winced nor cried aloud.
> Under the bludgeonings of chance
> My head is bloody but unbowed.
>
> Beyond this place of wrath and tears
> Looms but the horror of the shade,
> And yet the menace of the years
> Finds and shall find me unafraid.
>
> It matters not how straight the gate
> How charged with punishments the scroll,
> I am the master of my fate,
> I am the captain of my soul.

The searching words of the sermon having been concluded, Daniel proceeded to explain the handwriting that still remained on the wall. It has been said that Daniel could read it because he knew his Father's handwriting!

The Aramaic words of the mystic message as transliterated into English were: *Mene, Mene, Tekel, Upharsin.* The words mean "numbered," "weighed," and "divided" or "broken." With the help of God, Daniel was able to put this together into a meaningful message.

Mene—the days of Belshazzar's reign were numbered and were, in fact, finished. The tenure of every earthly ruler is determined by God. He had decided that the king had reached his limit. What solemn words were these: "Belshazzar, your number is up!"

Tekel—Belshazzar had been weighed in the balance of God and found too light in view of the blessings God had bestowed upon him. He was "found wanting" because he had not fulfilled what God expected of him as an earthly ruler. He had misused his position and privileges and had failed to acknowledge and glorify God. Solemn words again, "Belshazzar, you did not measure up!"

Peres (singular form of the plural *upharsin*)—Belshazzar's kingdom would come to an end and be divided and taken over by the powerful coalition of the Medes and the Persians. After all, it is the message of this entire book that God does set up and bring down the kingdoms of this world (2:21). Solemn words again, "Belshazzar, your kingdom is to be broken up!"

No indication is given as to the reaction of the king or of the rest who crowded this vast hall. Apparently, they accepted the message as an authoritative word from the God of heaven. It was! The night of revelry and revelation became a night of retribution.

A NIGHT OF RETRIBUTION (5:30–31)

Judgment struck swiftly. The Babylonians may have thought, "It can't happen to us!" But it did, and the account is told with graphic simplicity by the prophet Daniel: "In that night was Belshazzar the king of the Chaldeans slain. And Darius the Median took the kingdom, being about three-score and two years old" (vv. 30–31).

The fall of Babylon is also described in such ancient documents as the writings of Herodotus, Xenophon, and the *Nabonidus Chronicle*. These sources confirm that Babylon fell to the Persians quickly and without a major battle. The Euphrates River, which bisected the city, was diverted temporarily to a new channel, and the Persian soldiers then used the riverbed to enter and capture the city. Herodotus describes the climax: "[By] reason of the great size of the city . . . those in the outer parts of it were overcome, yet the dwellers in the middle part knew nothing of it; all this time they were dancing and making merry at a festival . . . till they learnt the truth but too well."

This intriguing chapter not only records the fulfillment of many prophecies pertaining to the Babylonian Empire but also seems to foreshadow the final doom of Gentile world power.

Dr. John Walvoord states: "In many respects, modern civilization is much like ancient Babylon, resplendent with its monuments of architectural triumph, as secure as human hands and ingenuity could make it, and yet defenseless against the judgment of God at the proper hour. Contemporary civilization is similar to ancient Babylon in that it has much to foster human pride but little to provide human security. Much as Babylon fell . . . so the world will be overtaken by disaster when the day of the Lord comes"

(*Daniel* [Chicago: Moody Press, 1971], 131). Our world seems as tragically oblivious to the warnings and portents of doom as the inhabitants of ancient Babylon.

In addition, the chapter illustrates the judgment individual sinners will face. *Eternity* magazine (February 1972) carried a story about a man who was arrested for and convicted of accepting policy bets on the telephone. Police had photographed him from a distance as he wrote his records on the wall of a house with a pencil. The blown-up photograph of the record on the wall, his handwriting, and the telephone numbers he used were all in the record. Many people might have looked upon him as a loiterer and his scribbling as nothing more than doodling, but there it was, and he went to jail.

Most people who sin do not write the record on a wall, but it is written just as plainly in the books of God, and His divine finger has written on another wall, "Thou art weighed in the balances and found wanting" (Dan. 5:27). They will meet their sins someday because they have written them where they will be brought to light. The only escape is to find forgiveness in Jesus Christ "in whom we have redemption through His blood, the forgiveness of sins, according to the riches of His grace" (Eph. 1:7).

Also noteworthy is the emphasis on the failure of Belshazzar to fulfill his stewardship, his mission on earth. God had graciously given him his kingdom and the very breath of life—but, as Daniel charged, the king did not glorify God (v. 23). He completely disregarded his Creator.

Modern man, like Belshazzar, has lost his way because he lacks a purposeful relationship with God and does not know why he is alive. A university professor declared, "Men have lost the sense of the purpose of being."

A Christian psychiatrist stated, "The main reason people see a psychiatrist is because they do not have any purpose in life."

After the acquittal of the Chicago Seven, one of them shouted, "Who will join me in trying to find the real purpose in life?"

Here it is: The real purpose of life is to glorify the God who gives and sustains physical life and who provides eternal life through Jesus Christ (John 3:16).

Jesus said to the Father, "I have glorified Thee on the earth" (John 17:4). And Paul exhorts believers, "For ye are bought with a price: therefore glorify God in your body" (1 Cor. 6:20).

Are you fulfilling your mission in life?

5—THINK IT OVER

As governments struggle for power throughout the world, we must be constantly aware of one overarching truth—God is the supreme, eternal Ruler of all nations, and His Word is utterly trustworthy. Whether or not these truths are acknowledged, He alone is sovereign, "removing kings and setting up kings." Our purpose as created beings is to glorify the King of kings.

1. Daniel 5:25–28 foretold the destruction of the kingdom of Babylon and it was confirmed in a creative message from God at Belshazzar's feast. What Aramaic words were written on the wall, and how did Daniel interpret their meaning to the king?

2. In relating the prophecies of Jeremiah 50–51, Isaiah 44:24–28, and 45:1–25 to the New Testament passages in 2 Timothy 3:16–17 and 2 Peter 1:20–21, what can you conclude about the trustworthiness of the Scriptures?

3. What does Daniel 5 teach about judgment? (See Eccl. 12:13–14; John 3:16–19, 36; 5:24, 27–29; Acts 10:42; Rom. 5:1; 8:1; 14:10; 1 Cor. 3:12–14; Rev. 20:11–15.)

4. Using these same references, distinguish between God's judgment on unbelieving sinners and the judgment that the Christian faces.

5. What three charges leveled against Belshazzar led to his downfall? (5:22–23).

6. Do we know non-believers in one of these stages of rebellion? What is our responsibility to them?

7. Evaluate this statement: "Man's chief end is to glorify God and to enjoy Him forever."

8. Define the term *glorified*. How is God glorified in the life of a believer?

9. How can Christians elevate the reputation of God in the eyes of others? How can we tarnish it?

10. Are you fulfilling God's plan for your life?

Reread Sara Teasdale's poem (text, p. 82). We cringe in the face of such blatant atheism. Teasdale apparently privately resists any inner prompting of the Spirit and defiantly proclaims her unbelief to the world. Should believers stand idly by while scoffers wield their pens and tongues to glorify Satan rather than God?

6

How to Tame Lions

The writer of an unsigned editorial in a respected secular magazine asked the following question: "Why so much unhappiness, unrest, and violence in the midst of so much material abundance? Why the low morale . . . the sense that things have gone wrong?" The writer then answered his own question: "All of these phenomena are related in one way or another to a single underlying condition—the loss of what might be called the invisible means of support, the inner resources that in earlier generations lent purpose to people's lives, connected them to the social order, restrained their conduct, and helped sustain them in adversity" (*Fortune,* April 1974).

The account of Daniel in the lions' den is of interest not only because it is one of the most familiar stories in the Old Testament but also because it sets before us the example of a man who possessed the "invisible means of support," the "inner resources" that gave purpose to his life, molded his conduct, and sustained him in adversity. Contemporary man would do well to study again this well-known episode and learn the secrets of living happily in a stress-filled society.

We will follow Daniel through this chapter as he is favored by Darius, framed by his enemies, faithful to Jehovah, thrown to the lions, and freed by the king.

DANIEL FAVORED BY DARIUS (6:1–3)

With the Persians in control of Babylon and the surrounding territory, it was appropriate for the new king to reorganize the government. But who was this new ruler called Darius? Since his name is not mentioned outside the Old Testament, some assume he was a fictional character and that this therefore constitutes "the most serious historical problem in the book." But how strong a case can be built on the silence of extrabiblical evidence, especially with new historical discoveries continually being made and with the consistent witness of archeology to the accuracy of Scripture? Besides, satisfactory solutions to the problem have been proposed. Biblical scholar D. J. Wiseman of the British Museum identifies Darius the Mede with Cyrus the Persian and translates Daniel 6:28, "In the reign of Darius, even in the reign of Cyrus the Persian." John C. Whitcomb in his book, *Darius The Mede,* argues persuasively on the other hand that Darius the Mede was Gubaru, whom Cyrus appointed to be governor over Babylon immediately after the fall of the city.

In the new administration 120 officials were appointed and set over the conquered area to hold down rebellion and to collect taxes. These officials were responsible to "three presidents" who in turn answered directly to the king (v. 2).

Daniel not only survived the downfall of Babylon but was given a high position in the new administration as one of the three presidents. Further, he distinguished himself in that position by working hard and well, and by displaying an excellent attitude. Darius took note of all this and planned to elevate the aged prophet still further to be a sort of prime minister of the whole realm.

Daniel's high position was not an accident of history. God wanted him in such a place at this crucial time, for the seventy-year captivity of the Jews would soon end and Daniel was in a position to influence King Cyrus regarding their return. The fact that the decree was so favorable to the Jews suggests that Daniel did have a part in it. (See Ezra 1:2–4; 6:3–5.)

God never leaves Himself without a witness. By His providence godly men are sometimes promoted to high offices in business and government. But whether the position the child of God occupies is high or low, he should perform conscientiously as Daniel did in his work while also seeking to forward the program of God.

DANIEL FRAMED BY HIS ENEMIES (6:4–9)

Not surprisingly, jealousy reared its ugly head among the presidents and princes, and it was directed against Daniel. His efficiency and integrity, as well as his favor with Darius, created what Daniel's co-workers thought was an intolerable situation. No doubt a secret meeting was held in which a strategy was adopted to find some pretext or cause to lay charges against Daniel to the king.

First, the officials scrutinized Daniel's professional life (v. 4). Was he conscientious, honest, hard-working? Hard as they tried, the investigators found no evidence of corruption, no basis in fact for any charges, and reluctantly concluded Daniel was faithful and trustworthy.

Next, the presidents and princes watched Daniel in his personal life. They followed him after business hours. What kind of company did he keep? What type of places did he frequent? The pursuit was fruitless. They found no "error or fault . . . in him" (v. 4).

Alexander McLaren described the court of Darius where Daniel worked as "half shambles and half pigsty. Luxury, sensuality, lust, self-seeking, idolatry, ruthlessness, cruelty, and the like were the environment of this man. And in the middle of these there grew up that fair flower of a character, pure and stainless, by the acknowledgment of enemies, and in which not even accusers could find a speck or a spot. There are no circumstances in which a man *must* have his garments spotted by the world. However deep the filth through which he has to wade, if God sent him there, and if he keeps hold of God's hand, his purity will be more stainless by reason of the impurity round him" (*Expositions of Holy Scripture* [London: Hodder and Stoughton, 1908], 69).

Eric Lund was star of the soccer team of the University of Connecticut and certain to be All-American. In his senior year, he was elected captain of the team with which he was never able to play. He died at the age of 22. His brave fight against leukemia gave him six "remissions" of the disease before the final round in which he fell.

For a young athlete who loved to "run the beaches," it was not easy keeping a will to live during his many extended periods in the hospital. During his final hospitalization, as death crept nearer, he whispered to his mother, "Do something for me. Leave a little early. Walk a few blocks and look at the sky. Walk in the world for me."

These words were imprinted on his memorial, which was erected by children of his hometown to whom he had given many hours of attention.

How similar to the words the Lord prayed in the presence of His disciples on that last night in the Upper Room. "As

Thou hast sent Me into the world, even so have I also sent them into the world" (John 17:18). Daniel "walked in the world" for God in his generation and set a noble example for God's people in all ages to do the same.

Finally, it was determined that no charge against Daniel could be concocted unless it pertained to his religious life (v. 5). And to this they now gave their earnest attention, proposing to Darius a new law, one they felt sure Daniel would break—and that would give them the means they sought to eliminate him.

The law they proposed was that no prayer or religious request be allowed for thirty days unless it was addressed to the king, on penalty of being cast into the den of lions. Further, as they urged the king to sign, these officials reminded him that, according to Medo-Persian law, a royal edict could never be revoked.

Not once suspecting the base motives of his leaders and flattered that they would propose such a law elevating him to the rank of deity, Darius hastily affixed his signature, and the matter became the law of the land.

DANIEL IS FAITHFUL TO JEHOVAH (6:10–15)

Daniel soon learned of the new law. His enemies saw to that. But he quietly and firmly made the decision to continue his habit of praying three times daily "as he did aforetime."

Did Daniel debate the alternatives? There were other options open to him. Why not cease praying for thirty days and outwit his enemies? Why not change his custom and pray elsewhere, perhaps in secret? Why not simply pray inaudibly as he went about his other duties? But, for Daniel, anything other than following his usual custom was subterfuge and would have involved loss of testimony before his enemies. He was not a man who served God only when there was no price to be paid.

Daniel's spirit reminds us of Polycarp, one of the Early Church fathers who was threatened with martyrdom in Smyrna if he did not reproach Christ. He replied, "Eighty and six years have I served Him, and He never did me any injury. How then can I blaspheme my King and Savior?"

And Daniel, too, was faithful to God though it appeared it would cost him his life. The plotters detected Daniel praying, just as they had anticipated (v. 11). Gleefully they hastened to the palace to make a report to the king, no doubt congratulating themselves along the way that everything was going according to plan.

First, the conspirators asked if the decree they had proposed had been signed into law and Darius assured them that it had (v. 12). Then the accusers sprang the trap on Daniel, charging that he had disregarded both the king and his decree (v. 13). They did not refer to Daniel as one of the presidents but with disdain as one "of the children of the captivity of Judah"—a stranger and foreigner in their midst and even a member of a conquered people.

The king's reaction was not what these men had expected. Darius was highly displeased, for he saw immediately that he had been duped by these officials and that the life of his favorite minister (v. 3) was now in extreme danger. He moved quickly, for time was limited, to try and deliver Daniel. No doubt he called in the finest legal experts to find, if possible, a loophole in the law. But, like an animal caught in a net, the more he tried to extricate himself from the situation, the more binding it became.

Darius thus faced a great dilemma. His law decreed that Daniel be executed, but his love would have released him. So might we think of God's law and His love. His law decrees,

"The soul that sinneth it shall die" (Ezek. 18:4). Therefore, since all have sinned, all face death, eternal separation from God. Yet God's love reaches out to all men and would forgive them. How can it be done? God found a way! "For God so loved the world that He gave His only begotten Son" (John 3:16). Jesus Christ, God's Son, satisfied God's law by His death so that now God can be both just and the justifier of him who believes in Jesus (Rom. 3:26).

For Darius there was no way out. The officials pressed their case (v. 15) and the king realized he had no choice but to turn Daniel over to the executioners.

DANIEL FED TO THE LIONS (6:16–22)

Darius failed to deliver Daniel but expressed a fervent hope, perhaps as they stood at the mouth of the den, that Daniel's God would preserve his life. "Your God whom you constantly serve will deliver you" (v. 16 NASB).

Daniel was then cast into the pit, and the entrance was sealed, a measure probably enforced by the officials to ensure that no attempt would be made to release the victim.

And what about Daniel? How did he react in the face of this severe trial? While the account is silent, it seems apparent that he did not remonstrate with the Lord as many of us might have done. "Lord, this is not fair. After all, I have faithfully served you for nearly seventy years and surely deserve better treatment than this." Rather, he committed himself and his fate to God and courageously faced what seemed to be certain death.

One writer imaginatively recreates what may have been Daniel's experience:

As the guards closed the aperture and went their way, Daniel slid gradually to the floor of the den. The big lions that had come bounding from their caverns at the inflow of light, all stopped suddenly short as a steed reined up by a powerful hand on the bridle. The initial roars died away as they formed a solid phalanx and looked toward this man who stood in their den in easy reach. There was some snorting and a little whining, and some of them turned around and went back to their caverns. Others of the great beasts yawned and lay down on the floor, but not one made a move to advance toward their visitor.

"Thanks be unto Jehovah," breathed the prophet. "He hath stopped the mouths of these fierce beasts that they will do me no harm." He sat down on the floor of the den and leaned his back against the wall to make himself comfortable for the night. Soon two cub lions moved in his direction, not stealthily or crouching as though to make an attack, but in obvious friendliness, and one lay on each side of Daniel as though to give him warmth and protection in the chilly dungeon. Presently their mother, an old lioness, crept over and lay in front of the prophet. He gently stroked their backs as they each turned their heads and licked his hand. . . . Enclosed by the lioness and her cubs, the head of the patriarch was gradually pillowed on the back of one of the cubs as the four slept soundly in perfect peace and tranquillity. (The Prophet-Statesman, 206).

Interestingly, the narrative now follows neither the main character, Daniel, nor the nobles who were convinced they had seen the last of the pious prophet. It follows the king. He had a bad night—one with no food, no entertainment, and worse, no sleep (v. 18). The king probably rolled and tossed on his bed, reviewing all the events and circumstances that had led to Daniel's present plight and wondering whether he had left undone anything that might have overturned the plot.

At dawn Darius arose and, forgetting his kingly dignity, ran quickly to the den of lions. Hoping for the best but fearing the worst—that he would hear only the growl of the lions in response—he cried in a "lamentable voice" and asked Daniel if God had been able to deliver His servant. Of course, regardless of whether Daniel survived or perished in the lions' den, God was able to deliver. As illustrated in chapter 3 of this book, the believer acknowledges God's ability and power but submits to His will in every situation. Regardless of what happens, we have the confidence that "all things work together for good."

In Daniel's case, it was God's will to deliver him. The prophet explained, "My God hath sent His angel, and hath shut the lions' mouths, that they have not hurt me" (v. 22). It seems probable that the deliverer of the three Hebrew youths (3:25, 28) and of Daniel (6:22) is the same person, the Angel of Jehovah. Daniel not only spent the night in the company of the lions, but infinitely better, in the company of the preincarnate Son of God! It is difficult not to be curious about the conversation through the night hours!

DANIEL FREED BY THE KING (6:23–28)

The chapter moves to its end with the reporting of three significant events. First, Daniel is removed from the den, and the explanation for his miraculous deliverance is said to be "because he believed in his God" (v. 23). The writer of the Book of Hebrews was probably referring to this great event when he said that some "through faith . . . stopped the mouths of lions."

Next, in a bloody sequel, Daniel's direct accusers (probably not all 122 of them) were punished. Persian law, in contrast to the Mosaic Law (Deut. 24:16), required the punishment of the criminals' families as well as the guilty men. One by one they were pushed into the den, caught in midair, and devoured before they reached the floor. How great a miracle Daniel's deliverance was that he could spend an entire night with these ferocious creatures and not be scratched! It is also another fulfillment of God's promise to Abraham and his seed that He would bless the ones who blessed them and curse those who cursed them.

Finally, Darius issued a sweeping proclamation that all men "tremble and fear" before Daniel's God. It has been pointed out that Darius did not here repudiate his Babylonian gods or worship Daniel's God. Nonetheless, the proclamation is remarkable for what it contains about the person, kingdom, and words of the God of Daniel (vv. 26–27).

As if to emphasize once more the magnitude of the miracle, the chapter concludes with the words, "So this Daniel prospered in the reign of Darius, and [even] in the reign of Cyrus the Persian" (v. 28). The same Daniel who was unjustly accused, unfairly convicted, and who was cast into a den of hungry, voracious beasts was still alive and prospering. Only the intervening hand of the living God could accomplish that!

It is not difficult to discover timely truths from this familiar chapter. But is it possible that our very familiarity with the story, perhaps from childhood on, has caused us to overlook those lessons that God intended us to learn from it? Certainly the chapter is not here simply to entertain. Let's take a closer look.

1. In terms of the broad purpose of the Book of Daniel—to portray God's dealings with the nations and with Israel to the time of the end—the events of this chapter would seem to foreshadow the final deliverance of Israel from her enemies and persecutors. This will be at the return of Christ to the earth. (See Zech. 14; Rev. 19:11–21.) At that time Israel will experience great deliverance physically and

spiritually, and the enemies of God and of His people will be judged and destroyed.

2. The character of Daniel fairly leaps out at us from these verses. Everything about him is exemplary—his integrity and the consistency of his life as a child of God (vv. 4–5); his stark courage (v. 10); his singular faith (v. 23); his discipline and devotion (v. 10). Says Leon Wood, "To have maintained such a demanding prayer schedule as this, even apart from continuing it now in the face of penalty, required great discipline of life. In his position as president, Daniel carried heavy responsibility, with much work to do. Under such demands the temptation to neglect this sort of prayer-program was no doubt strong, especially since he had to return home each noon for the purpose, while keeping on also with the morning and evening occasions. But Daniel had maintained it, apparently recognizing the priority of this faithful contact with God. He continued the same in the face of the unfair decree" (*A Commentary on Daniel* [Grand Rapids: Zondervan Publishing House, 1973], 163).

Daniel's priority list had fellowship with God at the top. This explains in large measure the godly life and character of this man. What is at the top of your priority list?

3. The people of God today are not exempt from the "lions' den" and need to be reminded again that God is able to deliver from "lions of adversity." Faith is the key. The Book of Hebrews declares, "But without faith it is impossible to please Him, for he that cometh to God must believe that He is, and that He is a rewarder of them that diligently seek Him" (Heb. 11:6). Faith is essential, but the faith must be in God.

Sir Don Campbell, the British car and boat racer, lost his life while racing a fast boat on one of the deep lakes in

Scotland. The boat exploded and rapidly sank. The only thing that ever surfaced was a toy stuffed animal, Campbell's "good luck charm" that was powerless to help him in the final and fatal crisis of his life.

One writer reminds us that the "lions" we confront "may be illness, business reverses, slander, domestic friction, or any of a great number of things. . . . When he faces the 'lions,' a Christian businessman who has encountered reverses, or a farmer who has lost a crop does not yield to despair but praises God for reminding him to lay up treasures in heaven. A Christian mother whose baby is snatched away by sudden death is not frantic, but is comforted by her assurance that she will rejoin her child in her Father's house. A young believer whose love is not returned is not embittered but quietly trusts that God acts in the best interests of His people" (*Bible Knowledge: Daniel* [Wheaton, Ill.: Scripture Press Publications, 1968], 73).

What "lions" are you facing? Do you believe God is able to deliver you? Are you willing also to surrender to God's will regardless of what happens, knowing and believing that "all things work together for good" (Rom. 8:28)?

A mother and father in New England felt the call of God to the mission field. When they told their three children, two responded excitedly but the middle child, a boy in his early teens, said, "I won't go! You'll have to go without me because I want to live in this town. This is the best place in all the world to live!" Then he ran upstairs to his room and sobbed for an hour. Finally, the mother went up to comfort him and opened the door of his room just as the boy began to play on his trumpet, with tears streaming down his face, "I Surrender All." Whatever it involves, God's will *is* best.

6—THINK IT OVER

This chapter is a powerful reminder that God is a miracle-maker! Yet, while we may identify Daniel with the incident in the lions' den more than with any other, we are learning that the prophet consistently demonstrated Christian character and commitment throughout his life. Here, however, is an object lesson on developing faith in God's power to deliver from adversity.

1. What was the cause of Daniel's distinction in the secular society of Babylon?

2. What motivated Daniel's enemies to seek his life?

3. How did King Darius react to the report that Daniel had failed to obey his edict? (See 6:3, 15–16.)

4. Trace the king's actions from the time Daniel was thrown into the den of lions until he was delivered.

5. How was Daniel's faith in God manifested in chapter 6?

6. What does it mean to have faith? (See Heb. 11; Eph. 2:8–10; John 1:12; 3:36.)

7. How is faith related to works? (See James 2:14–26.)

8. In what way was Daniel's commitment to prayer a preparation for facing this crisis? How should 1 John 5:14–15 and James 4:14–15 be incorporated into the prayer life of a Christian?

9. What "lions" might contemporary Christians be called upon to face? Consider memorizing the following Scripture verses for such times: Luke 18:1; Eph. 6:18; Phil. 4:6; 1 Thess. 5:17.

10. At what future time shall the "lion lie down with the lamb" and peace be restored to Israel? (See Zech 14; Rev. 19:11–21.)

Daniel's deliverance from the lions was in keeping with God's will for his life. God would use this miraculous deliverance as a witness to the king and to preserve Daniel for future ministry. Such times of divine intervention are faith-builders for all God's servants who walk in dangerous times and places.

7

History's Animal Parade

Dr. Margaret Mead appeared before the Washington Press Club to discuss the topic, "American Culture and the Future of the Family." Her audience was startled by her opening remarks: "Our first agenda is: Are we going to survive at all? The major struggle of marriage is who takes out the garbage. Does it matter who takes out the garbage if we're not going to be here? Are we going to be here? It's very doubtful. The whole world is in terrible danger" (*The Dallas Morning News,* April 6, 1976).

Dr. Linus Pauling, Nobel prize-winning scientist, has said that he is afraid that the greatest catastrophe in the history of the world will occur in the next twenty-five to fifty years. He said that he is nonetheless an optimist and believes the human race might survive!

What does the future hold? Is there any way for man to know? God alone knows the future, of course, and He has revealed in the Bible all that man needs to know about coming events.

When one of the great highway tunnels was built in Colorado, the work began at both ends simultaneously. When the crews met they were only one-half inch off center—and that was regarded as a remarkable engineering feat. The prophecies in the Bible, however, are more accurate than this, for theirs is not a relative but an absolute perfection. They will never miss the mark! Peter wrote, "We have the prophetic word made more sure" (2 Peter 1:19 NASB).

The Book of Daniel contains many of the key prophecies of Scripture, largely because the prophet Daniel "had understanding in all visions and dreams" (Dan. 1:17). He not only interpreted the dreams of others but also received four visions from God regarding future events. All four visions apparently occurred during the historical period covered in Daniel 1–6.

The first vision of Daniel is recorded in Daniel 7 and took place in the first year of the reign of Belshazzar, the last king of Babylon, about 555 B.C. The second is found in Daniel 8 and happened in the third year of Belshazzar's reign, about 552 B.C. Vision three is found in Daniel 9 and occurred about 538 B.C. in the first year of the reign of Darius the Mede. The fourth and final vision, the last recorded event of Daniel's life, is recorded in chapters 10 through 12 and took place in 536 B.C. in the third year of the reign of Cyrus.

Daniel 7 concludes the first major section of the book, which describes the destinies of the nations of the world. With chapter 8 we turn a corner and find the emphasis to be on the destiny of the nation of Israel.

At first glance there seems to be a remarkable similarity between the prophecies of chapters 2 and 7. Both give a panoramic sweep of Gentile world history, showing that there will be four great empires, each succeeding the other, and that history will come to its climax when God's kingdom is established on earth and His Son reigns.

But if this is true, why should it be necessary to cover the same ground twice? The answer is found not in the similarities between the two chapters but in the differences. The vision of chapter 2 was seen by a pagan king and therefore portrayed history as man would view it, each empire having at least some intrinsic value. The vision of chapter 7, however, was given to a man of God, and to him God reveals the nations of history as they really are inwardly. They are portrayed as God sees them—wild, ferocious beasts, continually fighting and devouring one another.

Further, Daniel 7 adds important information not found in chapter 2 about a wicked world ruler in the end times, and this information provides a foundation for the development of this personage's character and career in subsequent visions.

It has been said that chapter 7 "provides the most comprehensive and detailed prophecy of future events to be found anywhere in the Old Testament" (Walvoord, *Daniel*, p. 145). Clearly then, this is a chapter that merits our close attention.

THE DESCRIPTION OF THE VISION (7:1–14)

This first of four visions granted to Daniel came in the "first year of Belshazzar king of Babylon." Since Nebuchadnezzar was still king in chapter 4 and Belshazzar was in his last year as king in chapter 5, it is clear that the vision occurred between the episodes of these chapters. Daniel responded by writing down an account of what he saw and heard that night.

The four beasts (vv. 2–8). In his vision, Daniel first saw a "great sea" agitated by the "four winds of heaven." Out of this sea came successively four beasts, each different from the other. It is often suggested that the "great sea" represents the Mediterranean and that at one time or another each of the empires here described bordered on that sea. But those beasts (kings) were described as arising out of the earth (v. 17). It is better, therefore, to take the sea as a symbolic reference to nations. (See Isa. 57:20; Rev. 17:15.) The nations are here seen in perpetual turmoil and unrest, a not inaccurate picture as the annals of human history reveal. Out of the restless sea of people and nations, four beastlike kingdoms appear. These kingdoms can be identified by references within the Scriptures and are verified by secular history. It gives us a picture of human history as God sees it, a picture that is neither appealing nor attractive.

The first beast to appear was like a lion (v. 4), symbolizing the Babylonian Empire (612–539 B.C.). This corresponds with the identification of the head of gold (2:38). The national symbol of Babylon was a winged lion and many such statues have been discovered in the ruins of that ancient city. The wings are a focus of interest, symbolizing the swiftness of the conquests of a strong and cruel kingdom. The fact that the wings were torn out, that the lion was made to stand upright like a man, and that the heart of a man was given to it shows the dramatic change that came over this empire. No doubt this refers to the fact that Nebuchadnezzar, following his period of insanity and subsequent conversion to faith in Jehovah, became more humane in his manner of rule.

The second beast was like a bear (v. 5) and symbolizes the Medo-Persian Empire (539–331 B.C.), the identification of which is confirmed in Daniel 5:28, 31. It was predicted that Babylon would fall to Medo-Persia. The fact that the bear was raised up on one side indicates that Persia would gain ascendancy over Media and dominate as the superior power. The three ribs in its mouth probably symbolize Persia's conquests over Babylon, Lydia, and Egypt, carried out with its huge armies under the able direction of Cyrus. But the bear's appetite was not satisfied and she conquered more nations, devoured more empires. Persia, in fact, extended her conquests till her kingdom reached from the Indus River on the east to the land of Egypt and the Aegean Sea on the west.

The third beast to appear was like a leopard (v. 6) and symbolizes the Grecian Empire under Alexander and his successors (331–63 B.C.). This identification is confirmed in chapter 8 (vv. 20–22) and shows that Persia would be defeated by Greece. The leopard, a swift, cunning, and cruel animal with an insatiable thirst for blood, accurately symbolizes Alexander and his conquests. The four wings of the leopard denote unusual speed, a notable characteristic of the expansion of the Grecian Empire. The four heads of the beast logically and historically represent the division, among four of his generals, of Alexander's empire after his death.

The expression "dominion was given to it" is most interesting and significant. Did Alexander imagine that it was his military genius alone that enabled him and his small army of 35,000 men to defeat the massive hordes of the Persians numbering, some believe, in the millions? It is true that Alexander was a great leader, but his victories and subsequent dominion over a great empire were his because God, in the execution of His plans, allowed it to happen. Will world rulers ever understand this important fact?

The fourth beast to appear (v. 7) is not identified with any known animal. It has been said that no animal in the kingdom of beasts is so fierce and terrible as to portray this kingdom. The Apostle John apparently described the same beast (Rev. 13:1–10), saying it was like the leopard, bear, and lion in its features, incorporating elements from the previous empires into this one. The dominant feature of this beast and the empire it symbolized was its great and destructive strength, emphasized by several expressions in verse 7. This beast, it would appear, could only symbolize the Roman Empire, whose mighty iron legions of cruel and vindictive soldiers conquered the world of its day.

But there are more developments concerning the Roman Empire. Daniel saw that this beast representing Rome had ten horns on its head. He observed further that another "little horn" appeared abruptly, gained strength quickly, uprooted three other horns, and then spoke boastfully (v. 8).

What can these things mean? Since this is a question Daniel himself would raise and have answered in the latter part of the chapter, suffice it to say here that Daniel was describing things that are yet to be fulfilled. Despite the efforts of some interpreters to find fulfillment of these developments in history, their views have been shown to be faulty and inaccurate. The only correct interpretation must be that, since there is no historical fulfillment of these things, the time is still future when the Roman Empire will reappear. Then ten rulers will reign contemporaneously. Among them one will appear who, conquering three others, will eventually dominate the entire empire and finally become world dictator. He will be arrogant and boastful but will come to his end at the return of Christ to the earth.

The Ancient of Days (vv. 9–14). Abruptly the scene shifts from earth to heaven, from Satan's prodigy—the "little horn"—to the Ancient of Days, and from the arrogant blasphemies of Antichrist to the worship of angels before the throne of God!

The previous section of the vision has carried us to the end of time, the Tribulation, to the flowering of Satan's evil genius. In order that we may gain a heavenly perspective on these things, we are given a brief glimpse into glory to assure us that, after all, God is in control. The same is true of the companion Book of Revelation. In Revelation 4 and 5 we are transported to heaven because we must see that God is on His throne. He is the center of the universe. He is sovereign—and it is He who will execute judgments on evil, judgments that are fully described in Revelation 6–18.

The scenes and personages of Daniel's vision are graphically portrayed. First, there is the awesome vision of the Ancient of Days, no doubt God the Father. This, says one writer, is the only verse in all the Bible in which God the Father is depicted in human form (v. 9). His holiness, eternity, and glory are symbolically described. Before Him innumerable saints and angels minister and worship while books are opened and a judgment is set (v. 10).

Next, the scene shifts to one who is to be judged, the beast, or Antichrist. His body is to be "given to the burning flame," an obvious parallel to the prophecy (Rev. 19–20) that describes the beast being cast into the lake of fire.

Finally, the scene turns to the One who will carry out the sentence of judgment—"one like the Son of Man." This can be none other than the Lord Jesus Christ, the eternal Son of God, who often referred to Himself as the Son of Man and who described His Second Coming in the language of this verse (Matt. 24:30; 26:64). In fact, Caiaphas, the Jewish high priest, seemed to make the connection between Jesus' claims and this prophecy of Daniel and reasoned that Jesus was thus claiming the prerogatives of deity and was guilty of blasphemy.

In this vision Daniel saw the Son of Man approaching the Ancient of Days (v. 13). Why does He do this? It is recorded that the Father had said to the Son, "Ask of Me and I shall give Thee the [nations] for Thine inheritance, and the uttermost part of the earth for Thy possession" (Ps. 2:8). Now, as the Son anticipates His return to earth, He says, "Father give Me My inheritance!" And the inheritance is granted— "And there was given him dominion and glory, and a kingdom" (v. 14). The Son will come to judge His foes, claim His inheritance, and reign forever. (See Rev. 11:15.)

A missionary from Japan stated that during World War II Japanese military police visited Japanese churches and took the pastors and elders to court. They asked them two questions:

1. Do you believe that Jesus Christ will return the second time as the Bible teaches?

2. After Jesus Christ returns, do you believe the Emperor will worship Jesus Christ or that Jesus Christ will worship the Emperor?

There can be no confusion about the answers to such questions in the light of this passage.

THE MEANING OF THE VISION (7:15–27)

To this point there has been an objective, dispassionate report of Daniel's first great vision. Now, however, the prophet reveals his reaction to the momentous events he has seen portrayed. He is grieved and troubled and he seeks help in understanding these things from one of the angels who stands before God's throne (v. 16; see v. 10). The help is readily given: first, in summary fashion; then, in greater detail.

In summary (vv. 17–18). The angel tells Daniel the four beasts represent four kings "which shall arise out of the earth." The history of the four kings and their kingdoms is considered a unit, completed only when the last empire will be destroyed. Thus, though different imagery is used, the

empires described are the same as those in chapter 2—
Babylon, Medo-Persia, Greece, and Rome.

But ultimately, the "saints of the Most High shall take the
kingdom" (v. 18). This must be the fifth kingdom, the one
just granted to the Son of Man (v. 14), the kingdom He will
come to establish on earth. The saints, the saved of all ages,
will enter and enjoy to the full the time of Christ's reign.
Their position is to be the opposite of what would be characteristic of the previous kingdoms, for then evil would
dominate and evil men reign.

In 1776, American preachers, politicians, and many
ordinary citizens interpreted this chapter as applying to
America, particularly the promise that the "saints of the
Most High shall receive the kingdom" (v. 27). Evidence
seems clear that our forefathers saw themselves as a nation
with a millennial destiny. In 1771, Timothy Dwight, for
instance, wrote a hymn, "America," which expresses this
fond ideal:

> Hail Land of Light and Joy! Thy power shall grow
> Far as the seas, which round thy regions flow;
> Through earth's wide realms thy glory shall extend,
> And savage nations at thy scepter bend.

But America has not and will not launch God's kingdom
of justice and plenty. For that, we await the climactic and
glorious return of Jesus Christ.

In detail (vv. 19–27). Not entirely satisfied, Daniel asks
for more information from the angelic interpreter about the
intriguing four beasts and that mysterious "little horn."
Recapitulating the particulars for which he sought explanation, the prophet awaits the angel's response. Again the
messenger grants an answer.

"The fourth beast" represents the fourth kingdom, namely the Roman Empire (v. 23).

"The ten horns" symbolize ten rulers that will arise out of the region once controlled by Rome (v. 24). The kings will all rule at the same time, a phenomenon not to be found in the past. It is to be expected, therefore, that the Roman Empire in this form will reappear and that the ten rulers will be in power in the end times. (See Rev. 13:1; 17:12.)

"Another shall rise after them." Another ruler, in addition to the ten and different from them, will rise to power (v. 23). This is the "little horn" (v. 8), popularly called the Antichrist. His career is briefly described.

1. He will first conquer three of the ten rulers. This is how Antichrist will rise to power. He will come from one of the countries of the revived empire, according to Daniel's vision, and forcefully subdue three of the ten kings to become head of this Western federation of nations.

2. He will speak out against the true God of heaven (v. 25). The language indicates literally that he will attempt to raise himself to the level of God and make declarations from that supposed position. The Apostle Paul predicts the same of this evil personage (2 Thess. 2:4).

3. He will persecute the saints (v. 25). Though believers of the present age will be removed from the earth at the coming of Christ for the church (John 14:1–3; 1 Thess. 4:13–18), many people will believe in Christ and be saved in the Tribulation that follows (Rev. 7). For the believers, life will be difficult and even treacherous, particularly after Antichrist has come to power. He will harass, afflict, and persecute them without mercy and many will be martyred for their faith. The suffering of the saints will be particularly severe during the last half of the Tribulation, a period of three and one-half years.

4. He will attempt to change moral and natural laws of the universe, apparently without success (v. 25). An example of this may be seen in the attempt made by the leaders of the French Revolution to replace the seven-day week established by God with a ten-day week. Their efforts failed. On the other hand, Antichrist, energized by Satan, will be able to perform miracles that will cause many to accept his blasphemous claims and become his ardent followers (2 Thess. 2:8–11).

5. His career will come to a sudden and disastrous end (vv. 26–27). The angel concludes his interpretive remarks by describing the fate of Antichrist, the "little horn" (v. 11), and the establishment of a glorious kingdom on earth that the saints will inherit. This is the kingdom of the Son of Man (v. 14), to be realized in the earthly, millennial reign of Jesus Christ. Thus, Satan's counterfeit king and kingdom will be destroyed at Christ's coming to earth and the true King and kingdom will be established.

At the headquarters of the United Nations in New York City, a portion from the Book of Isaiah is inscribed on a marble wall: "They shall beat their swords into plowshares, and their spears into pruning hooks: nation shall not lift up sword against nation, neither shall they learn war anymore" (2:4).

But why was the first part of the verse omitted? After all, it tells how these blessings of peace and prosperity among nations are to be achieved! "And He [God] shall judge among the nations, and shall rebuke many people."

Is there a solution to earth's problems? Can we ever expect to see permanent peace on earth? The Scriptures give us a positive answer but affirm that the solutions to our problems will not come by the efforts of man in any World Court, League of Nations, or United Nations. The permanent solution will come when God intervenes once again in human history by sending His Son Jesus Christ to judge and to reign on this earth.

THE EFFECT OF THE VISION (7:28)

The chapter concludes with Daniel's brief statement describing his reaction to the angel's words of interpretation. Again, as at the close of the vision itself (v. 15), the prophet is troubled and deeply distressed. There is so much to grasp, and he pales at the thought of the rise of a vicious ruler who will cause great suffering among the people of God. Keeping the matter to himself, he continues to reflect on all that he has seen and heard, accepting as truth even that which he cannot understand—an attitude many of us will no doubt need to adopt regarding some of the matters in this and succeeding chapters of the Book of Daniel.

We are told that, among the scribes, Daniel 7 was considered the greatest chapter in the Old Testament. Without question, it teaches some basic and understandable things regarding God, man, and human history:

1. In the first place, though men glory in the advances and achievements of civilization through the centuries, God clearly sees human history as a chronicle of immorality, brutality, and depravity. Governments and governmental leaders may mask their true character from people for a time, but they are always unmasked before God. He always knows what man really is.

2. Again, human history will not continue indefinitely on its present course, nor will it come to an end with mankind annihilating itself in some great nuclear cataclysm. Things are in God's hands, not man's, and He has by no means abdicated as Lord of this universe.

3. Finally, human history will one day see again the inter-vention of God. Isaiah cried out in his time, "Oh that Thou wouldest rend the heavens, that Thou wouldest come down" (Isa. 64:1). John, in a vision, was carried forward to the Second Advent of Christ and recorded the answer to the prayer: "And I saw heaven opened, and behold a white horse; and He that sat upon him was called Faithful and True, and in righteousness He doth judge and make war" (Rev. 19:11).

Billy Graham has told of an interview with the late Konrad Adenauer, then Chancellor of West Germany. Mr. Adenauer asked Mr. Graham a series of questions:

"Do you believe Jesus Christ rose again from the dead?" Graham replied, "Yes, sir, I do."

"Do you believe He ascended and is in heaven now?"

"Yes, sir, I do."

"Some say Jesus Christ will return and reign on this earth. Do you believe that?"

"Yes, sir, I do."

After a brief pause, Mr. Adenauer said, "So do I. If He doesn't, there is no hope for this world!"

7—THINK IT OVER

With this chapter, containing many of the key prophecies of Scripture, we enter deep and difficult waters. Yet, as seen through the eyes of God's beloved prophet, the vision of the future takes on a less ominous prospect. God's view of history (chap. 7) is vastly more comforting—and accurate—than man's view (chap. 2). In Him, and Him alone, there is hope!

1. Since the following terms will be mentioned or inferred during the study of the remaining chapters of the Book of Daniel, take time to define them according to the Scriptures:

(a) *Rapture* —(See 1 Cor. 15:51–57; 1 Thess. 4:13–18.)

(b) *Tribulation* —(See Jer. 30:7; Rev. 6–19.)

(c) *Second Coming* —(See Zech. 14:1–5; Matt. 24:29–31; 2 Thess. 2:8–10; Rev. 19:11–21.)

(d) *Millennium* —(See 2 Sam. 7:12–16; Luke 1:31–33; Rev. 20:1–4.)

2. The personage described as the "little horn" in Daniel 7:8 is the Antichrist. Outline his character and activity as revealed in 7:7–8, 11, 20–26; 8:23–25; 9:26–27; 11:36–45.

3. What does Daniel 7:9–10 reveal about the character and activity of God the Son? Compare with Matthew 24:30; 26:64, and Revelation 11:15.

4. In considering God's view of history, what attribute does He possess that allows Him to make such accurate judgment concerning the nations? (See 1 John 3:3; Acts 15:18; 1 Sam. 2:3; Isa. 40:27–28.)

5. How does God's perspective of future events contrast with man's perspective? (See 1 Sam. 16:7.)

6. Which prophecies in Daniel 7 have already been fulfilled? (See vv. 8–14, 18, 21–27.)

7. What does Daniel 7 tell us about the Tribulation, the Antichrist, the Second Advent of Christ, the judgment on the Antichrist, and the millennial kingdom?

8. How does the believer know that history is unfolding according to God's plan?

9. How does God plan to intervene in history, according to 2 Peter 3:3–10?

10. What means is there for escaping the wrath of the Tribulation (see 1 Thess. 1:10; 5:9; Rev. 3:10) and the judgment of Christ (see 2 Thess. 2:8–12; Rev. 19:11–21).

If God knows history, then He also knows the heart of man. If God has a plan for history, then He has a design for the lives of believers. If God will intervene again in history, then Christians ought to live expectantly, in light of that great event!

8

Superpowers in Conflict

A retired United States Army colonel introduced himself after I had concluded a prophetic message at a church in a southwestern city. He seemed eager to tell his story.

Having been retired from the army for only a short time, he said that the last thing he did while still in the military was to participate in a mock staging of World War III. Joining other officers from the Pentagon, he left Washington, D.C., and went to a remote underground retreat, established to carry on the affairs of government in the event of a nuclear attack. There these military men staged the "final conflict" between the nations. They projected that it would begin with a nuclear exchange between Israel and the Arab nations. The great superpowers, the U.S.A. and Russia, would next be drawn in and, finally, the European nations would join the conflict. The ensuing worldwide nuclear warfare would result in the loss of 55 million lives in the U.S.A. alone. So shaken at the prospect was this Christian army officer that he resigned his commission and now spends his time trying to reach people, especially children, with the gospel before the end comes.

Daniel, too, is shaken as he sees in prophetic vision a coming conflict between two great powers. Clouds of doom are gathering, which portend deep trials for his own people, the Jews. In fact, Daniel 8 introduces a new section of the book, signaled by the return to the use of the Hebrew language. The earlier chapters (2:4–7:28) are in Aramaic, the language of the Gentile world of the day, because the material emphasizes the destinies of the Gentile nations— their rise, progress, decline, and collapse. Beginning with Daniel 8 and continuing through the remainder of the book, the emphasis is on the destiny of the people of Israel. The plight and fortunes of Israel are now traced through the period already discussed from a Gentile perspective. Now we are to study human history as it relates to Israel, and the original language of the text is appropriately Hebrew.

This is the second of Daniel's four visions, coming two years after the first, in 551 B.C. In the first (chap. 7), Daniel saw four world empires to which his people would be subject for long centuries—Babylon, Medo-Persia, Greece, and Rome. He now receives more knowledge concerning the second and third of these empires, Persia and Greece. The reason for this is clear: In the latter period of Grecian domination of Israel, a ruler would arise who would unleash terrible hatred against the Jews, again desolating Jerusalem and its rebuilt temple as Nebuchadnezzar had done.

THE DESCRIPTION OF THE VISION (8:1–14)

The setting of Daniel's vision is given in the opening verses. It came in the third year of Belshazzar's reign, before the fall of Babylon recorded in Daniel 5. Geographically, the prophet saw himself in the province of Elam at Shushan the palace (or fortress). Probably Daniel was actually in Babylon but was transported in vision to a place some 230 miles east of that city. Formerly the capital of the Elamite kingdom, Shushan was now an insignificant place; yet in the future it would be an important Persian capital, the home of Esther and of Nehemiah.

The ram (vv. 3–4). In this vision Daniel sees a ram nearby with the customary two horns. The unusual thing was that as Daniel watched, one horn grew and became higher than the other. Then the ram moved in three directions—west, north, and south. It was impossible, in fact, to stop the ram, for it was irresistible and "became great."

There can be no debate concerning the meaning of the symbol, for it is declared, "The ram which thou sawest having two horns are the kings of Media and Persia" (v. 20). Though Media was first the major power of the time, Persia, under Cyrus, soon gained control over it and went on to conquer kingdoms to the west, north, and south. In fact, Cyrus and his son Cambyses II were invincible and established the largest empire the world had seen to that day. But it was destined to fall.

The he-goat (vv. 5–8). As Daniel contemplates with amazement the conquests of the ram, another animal appears on the scene to challenge him—a "buck of the goats" with a conspicuous horn between his eyes. This goat moves so swiftly his feet do not touch the ground, and the suspense builds as he approaches the ram. A great clash produces an astonishing result—with no assistance to deliver him from the fury of the he-goat, the ram is totally defeated.

Not surprisingly, the goat then becomes very strong, but at the height of its strength and power there are shocking developments—the great or conspicuous horn is broken, and in its place four prominent horns appear and extend in four directions.

Again, we are grateful for the interpretive guides provided later in the chapter (vv. 21–22). There we are told that the goat represents Greece. Further, the "great horn" symbolizes the first king, namely, Alexander the Great, and the four horns that replace it represent the four kingdoms that follow and replace Alexander's dominion.

It was in 334 B.C. that Alexander the Great came "from the west" (v. 5), nursing a desire to avenge what the Persians had done in Greece some 150 years before. In that year he crossed the Hellespont and defeated the Persian armies under Darius III at the Granicus River. Freeing the Grecian cities of Asia Minor from the Persians, Alexander confronted Darius himself at the Cilician Gates of Syria, winning a second decisive victory at the Battle of Issus near Antioch in 333 B.C. Darius now offered to negotiate, but Alexander swept south to occupy Egypt after taking Tyre and Gaza in prolonged sieges. Retracing his steps through Syria, the conqueror met the Persians and defeated them a third time, even though they had amassed much larger and more powerful armies.

This climactic victory took place near the site of old Nineveh called variously Gaugemela or Arbella. The year was 331 B.C. when Alexander finally "cast him [the ram] to the ground and stamped upon him" (v. 7).

From there Alexander drove on to capture and sack the Persian cities of Shushan, Ecbatana, and Persepolis. Still continuing his conquest, he swept eastward to the land of India, but finally weary armies had had enough and he returned to Babylon where he died in 323 B.C. at the age of 33, a victim of a severe fever. Thus was fulfilled the scriptural prophecy, "when he was strong, the great horn was broken" (v. 8).

Alexander completely destroyed Persia as a world power and conquered the greatest amount of territory of any of history's kings or soldiers.

Finally, in a prophetic statement not to be fulfilled for many years, Daniel's vision predicts that Alexander's empire would fall into four divisions (v. 8). After over twenty years of struggle and infighting, Alexander's four generals assumed rule as follows: Cassander over Macedonia and Greece; Lysimachus over Thrace and most of Asia Minor; Seleucus over Syria and vast territory to the east; and Ptolemy over Egypt and possibly Palestine.

It was the emergence of a ruler out of the line of Seleucus that was to affect the fate of the Jews, and to that development we now turn.

The little horn (vv. 9–14). As Daniel's vision continues, he sees a "little horn" (a ruler) coming from one of the four horns (one of Alexander's generals).

Who is this "little horn" (v. 9)? There is general agreement that he is Antiochus IV Epiphanes, eighth in the line of successors from Seleucus, and that he reigned in Syria from 175–164 B.C. Thus, the prophecy skips from 301 B.C., the time of the division of Alexander's empire, to 175 B.C. when Antiochus Epiphanes became king.

Is he to be identified with the "little horn" of chapter 7? Clearly they are not the same, for the little horn of chapter 7 arises out of the Roman Empire in the end times, whereas the little horn of chapter 8 springs from the Grecian Empire in ancient times. But they are both called "horns," because a horn is symbolic of rulership and power. C. I. Scofield said in his *Notes* (Scofield Bible), "They are alike in hatred of the Jews and of God, and in profaning the temple." In fact, it seems clear that Antiochus Epiphanes, the enemy of the Jews in the intertestamental period, foreshadowed Antichrist, the enemy of the Jews in the Tribulation. What Antiochus did is a pattern for what Antichrist will do.

What was Antiochus's attitude toward the Jews? Rebuffed by the Romans on his second campaign into Egypt, Antiochus determined to unify all his people to withstand the Roman threat. In order to accomplish this, Greek culture and religion were imposed on all his subjects, including the Jews. Attempts were made to stamp out the Jewish religion. It became unlawful to read the Torah, observe the Sabbath, practice circumcision, etc. Those who disobeyed these edicts were massacred. In one assault on Jerusalem, forty thousand Jews were killed in three days and ten thousand more were carried into captivity. This seems to be the allusion of verse 10. It is possible that the awful fate of the Jews in this dark hour of their history is described in the Book of Hebrews (11:35–38).

How did Antiochus profane the temple? His evil activities with reference to the temple and temple worship are described in Daniel 8:11–12. From 1 and 2 Maccabees and the writings of Josephus, we learn the precise manner in which these prophecies were fulfilled. Antiochus systematically looted the temple of its treasures, even carrying off the golden altar of incense, table of shewbread, and golden lampstand. He then caused the daily sacrifice to cease (v. 11) by erecting an idol, probably of the supreme Greek god Zeus, and offering swine to it. Thus, the true religion involving the worship of Jehovah was "cast to the ground," and the false religion of paganism was substituted.

How long did such desecrations last? In essence this is the question Daniel overheard two "holy ones" (angels) discussing (v. 13)—a question that no doubt burned in the prophet's mind as well. How long, indeed, would the temple and the Jewish people be trampled underfoot by this madman? (He called himself Antiochus "Epiphanes"—the glorious one; the Jews bitterly referred to him as Antiochus "Epimanes"—the madman!)

The answer is that the persecutions and desecrations would last for 2,300 days (v. 14). Working from December 25, 165 B.C., the established date for the restoration and cleansing of the temple under Judas Maccabeus, 2,300 days brings us to September 6, 171 B.C., the apparent date for the beginning of Antiochus's oppression of the Jews.

It is the December 25, 165 B.C. date that Jews still celebrate with the Jewish feast of Hanukkah (meaning "dedication"). It is also called the Festival of Lights, in memory of the discovery of oil for the temple lamps, and Jews commemorate that glad day of the repossession of their temple by placing candles in the windows of their homes.

A persecutor of the Jews in Russia asked a Jewish man what he thought the outcome would be if the wave of persecutions continued. The Jew answered, "The result will be a feast! Pharaoh tried to destroy the Jews, but the result was the Passover. Haman attempted to destroy the Jews, but the result was the Feast of Purim. Antiochus Epiphanes tried to destroy the Jews, but the result was the Feast of Dedication."

THE MEANING OF THE VISION (8:15–26)

Daniel was perplexed by the vision and tried in vain to understand it. Small wonder. We have the advantage of comparing these prophecies with their historical fulfillment and still find them difficult to comprehend. What must it have been to try to grasp their meaning while all these things were still future? God understood Daniel's limitations, however, and sent Gabriel to give the interpretation, but the prophet was so overcome by the presence of a supernatural being that he fainted. Only when he was restored to consciousness could be hear the angel's explanation of the vision.

In order to provide a basis for an understanding of what was to follow, Gabriel twice explained the general reference of the vision. He said it was for "the time of the end" (v. 17) and repeated the thought again with the words, "It pertains to the appointed time of the end" (v. 19 NASB).

Now the meaning of these expressions is obviously crucial for an accurate understanding of the remaining verses. Some interpreters regard the "time of the end" as the period of Jewish sufferings under Antiochus Epiphanes, who reigned 175–164 B.C. and who persecuted the Jews 171–165 B.C. But that period did not in any sense mark an end to Jewish sufferings. Furthermore, the similarity between the career described in Daniel 8:23–25 and that of Antichrist depicted in Daniel 7:24–26 is unmistakable. It should also be noted that the expression "time of the end" occurs in Daniel 12:4 where it clearly means the time approaching Christ's Second Coming. The conclusion, then, is that we are to see in Antiochus Epiphanes a dread picture and symbol of Antichrist to come in the end time, or Tribulation period. While the chapter admittedly describes the evil character and deeds of Antiochus, "the Antichrist of the Old Testament," it is also clear that he foreshadows the Antichrist of the New Testament.

Prophecy sometimes has a double fulfillment. So here we are able to see the partial fulfillment of the vision in Antiochus and the complete fulfillment in Antichrist.

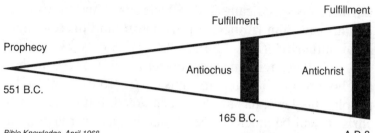

Fulfillment

Prophecy

Antiochus   Antichrist

551 B.C.

165 B.C.

Bible Knowledge, April 1968

A.D.?

Briefly, Gabriel identifies the ram and he-goat of the vision (vv. 20–21) and also the "great horn" and "four notable ones" that stand in its (Alexander's) place (v. 22). But the main burden of Gabriel's message concerns the "little horn," now referred to as a "king of fierce countenance." Let us observe what is said of this sinister character, keeping in mind that often both Antiochus and Antichrist are in view.

1. He will appear "in the latter time of their kingdom" (v. 23). The immediate context would relate this to the end of the rule of the divisions of Alexander's kingdom, near to the time when Rome would come to power. It was at that time that Antiochus Epiphanes seized the throne in Syria.

2. He will appear "when the transgressors are come to the full" (v. 23). The sins of the Jews after the Exile seem to be in view here. For this, God permitted the sharp oppressions under Antiochus which in turn foreshadow the deep trials of the yet future "time of Jacob's trouble."

3. He will be "a king of fierce countenance, and understanding dark sentences" (v. 23). Daniel is told that this ruler will be a foreboding person with a fierce manner and a brilliant mind capable of solving hard problems of his administration, facts true of both figures under discussion.

4. He will have great power due to satanic control (v. 24). Antiochus's inhuman conduct could only have been inspired by Satan. There would appear to be no other explanation. Further, it is specifically said of Antichrist, "And the dragon [Satan] gave him [Antichrist] his power, and his seat, and great authority" (Rev. 13:2).

5. He will exercise his great power to "destroy the mighty and holy people." That Antiochus destroyed many of God's people, the Jews, has already been noted. But under Antichrist it will be much worse. Jesus, in fact, warns Jewish believers in that future time of tribulation to flee the ravages of the "abomination of desolation," adding that "except those days should be shortened [terminated], there should no flesh be saved" (Matt. 24:22).

6. He will practice deceit to accomplish his purposes (v. 25). History confirms that Antiochus was a master in the art of deception, only to be exceeded by the Antichrist he preshadows. (See 2 Thess. 2:9–10; Rev. 13:12–14.)

7. He will exalt himself (v. 25). Again, we know this to be true of Antiochus, but it will be a trait even more prominently displayed by Antichrist. Paul wrote of this man of sin, "Who opposeth and exalteth himself above all that is called God, or that is worshiped so that he as God sitteth in the temple of God showing himself that he is God" (2 Thess. 2:4).

8. He will promise peace and security but will instead bring destruction (v. 25). This was a tactic practiced by Antiochus, according to 1 Maccabees: "And after two years' time the king [Antiochus] sent his chief collector of tribute into the cities of Judah; and he came into Jerusalem with a great multitude. And he spake words of peace unto them, in deceit; and they gave him credence. And he fell suddenly upon the city, and smote it very sore, and destroyed much

people of Israel" (1 Macc. 1:29–30). That Antichrist will duplicate the deception seems clear: "For when they shall say, 'Peace and safety,' then sudden destruction cometh upon them, as travail upon a woman with child; and they shall not escape" (1 Thess. 5:3).

9. He will oppose the "Prince of princes" (v. 25). According to verse 11, Antiochus would oppose God, the Prince of the Jewish host. But the expression used here, "Prince of princes," seems to be a direct reference to Christ, the Messiah. The one opposing Him will be Antichrist, his very name indicating his posture of antagonism toward the Son of God (Rev. 19:19).

10. He will be "broken without a human hand" (v. 25). While Antiochus died of grief in Babylon after his armies suffered defeat in battle, Antichrist will be broken by the intervention of Jesus Christ at the time of His return to the earth. His armies will be defeated and destroyed by the word of Christ, and Antichrist himself will be cast into the lake of fire (Rev. 19:20–21).

THE EFFECTS OF THE VISION (8:27)

Once again, prophetic insights into matters affecting Daniel's people in the future caused such a severe emotional reaction on the part of the prophet that he was sick for a number of days. Returning to his work in the court of Belshazzar, he could not shake his feelings of astonishment over the revelation he had received, nor could he understand its full significance.

Daniel took all of this very seriously—and so should we. No generation in history has had to face the problems our world now has to grapple with—an energy crisis, food shortages, environmental pollution, nuclear weaponry, etc. And world leaders are looking for someone—anyone—who can provide answers. The time is ripe for Christ to return and reign over this earth. Only He can solve the massive problems, both internal and external, that plague human society. But before the world sees Christ, they will embrace an Antichrist. He will promise deliverance—but he will lead the world to disaster!

A poem expressing, we fear, the attitude of many, was written by James Kirkup and read over the British Broadcasting Company in England as a birthday card for the Antichrist!

> Wherever now you are, and whoever you may be,
> In countryside or city, in the mountains or at sea,
> Dark with the vigor of the wave that bears our age,
> Or fair and impossible as my own lost image;
> You through the furnaces of all disaster
> Shall surely walk, and through the deserts of our day,
> Through the spirit's night, the mind's bright master
> You shall prove, and through the body's golden clay
> Shall breathe the soul, and draw the precious veins of
>   stone
> That burn to speech the dumbness of our flesh and bone.
> You, at the last, great savior, shall arrive, and be
> The one our insecurity confesses and awaits.
> For you alone can come, and take us seriously,
> With a gay abandon, we who at the gates
> Of nothing live with lust, and pride, and vanity, and war.
> May I, too, prince, now recognize for what you are
> You with the unknown face, and the familiar eyes
> Whose voice is all men's, and whose love is wise.
>   (Appeared in *Eternity* magazine, Jan., 1953)

But Antichrist and his followers will come to a bitter end. Only the believers in Jesus Christ will inherit eternal life and reign with Him. In view of the fact that we may be living nearer than we realize to the "time of the end," non-Christians should ponder carefully the words of Paul, "Behold, now is the accepted time; behold, now is the day of salvation" (2 Cor. 6:2). And Christians should heed his words which come at the end of a long discourse on prophetic matters: "Therefore, my beloved brethren, be ye stedfast, unmoveable, always abounding in the work of the Lord, forasmuch as ye know that your labor is not in vain in the Lord" (1 Cor. 15:58).

Dr. H. A. Ironside was to preach a prophetic message in a certain church. A godless man entered the service late and took a seat near the front. After the meeting this man approached Dr. Ironside and said, "I'm glad you agree with me."

"Oh, you hold to the Second Coming, do you?" asked the preacher.

"Oh, yes," was the quick reply.

"Well, does it hold you?"

The man was clearly taken aback. "What do you mean?" he asked.

"I mean has it gripped you—has it made a difference in your life?" explained Dr. Ironside.

The man shot back a retort, "Who has been telling you about me?"

All biblical truth, prophecy included, is intended to make the believer a mature person, fully equipped for good works. (See 2 Tim. 3:16–17.)

How has the study of the prophetic Scriptures affected you?

8—THINK IT OVER

Are times really so different since Daniel uttered his prophetic revelations? People are still stiff-necked and rebellious, or lethargic and apathetic. In either case, few will hear the warnings issued by a loving God. But for those who will study and apply prophecy to daily life, the rewards are infinitely worth the investment.

1. Read Daniel 8:3–14 and describe (or sketch) what you "see" and "hear."

2. What parts of the vision are interpreted by Gabriel in 8:19–26? How has the vision been fulfilled in the history of the Jews?

3. The Jewish people have suffered almost perpetual persecution. Which of these persecutions are recorded in Scripture? (See Exod. 1:18–22; Num. 22:2–6; 2 Kings 18:13–35.)

4. What modern persecutions have the Jews endured?

5. What happened to the persecutors of the Jews in Bible times? The judgments on Israel's persecutors are a fulfillment of God's promise to Abraham (Gen. 12:3).

6. What warning is there concerning one's treatment of the Jews? (See Matt. 25:31–46 where Christ's "brethren" are identified as the Jews.)

7. What does fulfilled prophecy indicate about God? His purposes? His Word?

8. What benefit is there to believers in having a knowledge of prophetic events? (See John 14:1–3.)

9. How should a knowledge of these events affect the conduct of believers? (See 1 Cor. 15:51–58; Phil. 3:20–4:1; Titus 2:11–13; 2 Peter 3:10–14.)

10. How should this knowledge affect a believer's treatment of the Jews? (See Gen. 12:3; Dan. 8:24–25; Matt. 25:31–46.)

In these days, as we near "the time of the end" with the prospect of the final confrontation between the forces of good and evil before us, there is something believers can do! We can heed the words of Paul: "Therefore, my beloved brethren, be ye stedfast, unmoveable, always abounding in the work of the Lord, forasmuch as ye know that your labor is not in vain in the Lord" (1 Cor. 15:58).

9

What's Ahead for Israel?

A seminary student who was also a pastor commented that he did not preach on prophecy because "prophecy distracts people from the present." One of his professors observed, "Then there is certainly a lot of distraction in the Scriptures!"

It has been well stated that prophecy is neither escapism nor a distraction from the present. Rather, for the Christian, it is motivation for the present. We see in this chapter how true this was for Daniel the prophet.

Daniel 9 has been called by one writer "the backbone of prophecy," and by another, "the high point of the Book of Daniel." As chapters 2 and 7 outline the prophetic program of the Gentile nations, so chapter 9 reveals God's prophetic program for the Jews. In fact, this chapter answers the very timely question, "Will Israel survive?"

A few years ago, a suburban area near one of our major cities was being developed as a very exclusive residential community. At first only a few Jewish people bought sites for homes; then more and more purchased lots. Other people in the community began to agitate to force the Jews out.

The minister of a nearby church announced as his sermon topic for the next Sunday, "How to Get Rid of the Jews." This caused a furor. Everyone in the area talked about it all week, and some Jews even protested to the governor of the state.

When Sunday came, the church was jammed with people. A Jewish rabbi and two reporters appeared and stalked to the front of the church. The pastor read his text: "Thus saith the Lord, which giveth the sun for a light by day, and the ordinances of the moon and of the stars for a light by night, which divideth the sea when the waves thereof roar. The Lord of hosts is His name. 'If those ordinances [sun, moon, and stars] depart from before Me,' saith the Lord, 'then the seed of Israel also shall cease from being a nation before Me for ever'" (Jer. 31:35–36).

With a smile on his face the rabbi turned to the reporters and said, "It's all right, boys!"

Yes, Israel will survive! God's program for her as a nation is revealed in Daniel 9. But the revelation came in answer to Daniel's intercession. This chapter then is a remarkable picture of a prophet at prayer.

THE OCCASION OF THE PRAYER (9:1–2)

Daniel's third vision came in 538 B.C., the first year of the Persian king Darius's rule and about the time of Daniel's experience in the lions' den. Busy as he was in his position with the new government, the prophet found time to pray three times a day (6:10) and to study the Scriptures (9:2).

In the providence of God, his attention at this time was focused on the scroll of Jeremiah and the prediction that the captivity of the Jews would have a duration of seventy years. If the beginning of the captivity is dated from the time of Daniel's deportation in 605 B.C. (there were other deportations in 597 and 586 B.C.), then 67 of the 70 years had elapsed, and Daniel realized he was living on the very threshold of the fulfillment of prophecy.

It is important to note that Daniel believed in the literal interpretation of prophecy. To him, the seventy years meant seventy actual years and were not to be symbolized or spiritualized in any way. Daniel obviously expected the exile to end soon and within the number of years the prophet Jeremiah had predicted. (See Jer. 25:11–12; 29:10.)

Significantly, living within the imminent fulfillment of an important prophecy (Israel's restoration to the land) did not distract Daniel nor prove to be a spiritual hindrance. Just the opposite happened, in fact. It drove him to his knees for a ministry of intercession on behalf of his people.

A Christian leader recently said, "I do not personally believe that the Lord's return is imminent. I think the current teaching that it is imminent is leading many, many Christians to fold their hands and disobey what Jesus said to do. Jesus said we should 'work, for the night is coming when no man can work.'"

Of course, some people respond improperly to prophetic teaching, but that does not invalidate what the Bible teaches about the future. Importantly, the Scriptures themselves use prophecy as the basis for spiritual exhortation.

Daniel, for one, was properly motivated by his awareness of prophetic revelation and fell to his knees to pray. But why should he pray when God had already promised to accomplish what he was praying for—the restoration of the Jewish people? First, because the Lord said in connection with the promise of the return, "'And ye shall seek Me, and find Me, when ye shall search for Me with all your heart. And I will be found of you,' saith the Lord, 'and I will turn away your captivity and I will bring you again into the place whence I caused you to be carried away captive'" (Jer. 29:13–14).

A foreboding may well have gripped Daniel's heart because, even though the time had come for the end of the Babylonian exile, the Jews were not seeking after God. Many of them were, in fact, too comfortable in Babylon to care about going back to Jerusalem. Daniel, therefore, prayed to Jehovah on their behalf. Like Moses in the wilderness, Daniel now became Israel's intercessor. Since they were not seeking God, Daniel did it for them as their representative.

In the second place, Daniel prayed because he felt he should claim God's promise. The great prayers of the Bible show that the saints of old reverently reminded God of His promises, laying hold of them for their immediate situation. We must learn to do the same.

Some years ago a seminary student met with his fellow classmates for a prayer meeting in the dormitory. Though he had memorized a great many Scripture verses, he seemed to have difficulty retaining them. As he prayed, he started to quote one of the great promises of God because he wanted to claim it for his own. But he soon began to stumble and stammer, forgetting the verse halfway through. Finally he said, "Just a minute, Lord!" Going over to his desk, he turned to the reference in his Bible and pointed to it. "Here it is, Lord, right here!" God's promises are challenges to prayer.

THE NATURE OF THE PRAYER (9:3–19)

This is one of the great intercessory prayers of the Bible. It is marked by humility (v. 3), worship (v. 4), confession of sin (vv. 5–14), and petition (vv. 15–19).

Clearly the emphasis of the prayer is on the sin of the Jews. Daniel earnestly sought God's forgiveness for them

so that there might be no delay in their return to their
homeland. Yet the prophet did not have a judgmental and
superior attitude toward his people but identified himself
freely with them and with the stigma of their sin. Nor did he
attempt in any way to excuse, evade, rationalize, or mini-
mize the offenses of the Jews. In a most straightforward
manner the prophet said to the Lord, "We have sinned, and
have committed iniquity, and have done wickedly, and
have rebelled, even by departing from Thy precepts and
from Thy judgments" (v. 5).

This forceful accumulation of verbs is a thorough confession that they were guilty of all kinds of sins. Further, all
levels of God's people are indicated—kings, princes, fathers,
and common people—all are guilty (v. 6). No one can be
excused.

And such sin brought its inevitable dire results. First,
Israel's sin brought the shame of the dispersion and captivity (vv. 7–8), and second, it brought the curse of God
upon them (v. 11). Surely Daniel had in mind such warnings as Leviticus 26:14–39 and Deuteronomy 28:15–68. In
the latter passage especially, God set before His people two
options: blessing for obedience or cursing for disobedience.
Choosing disobedience, Israel tasted the bitter curses and
learned that sin inevitably brings divine judgment.

It still does. The mills of God may grind slowly, but they
do "grind exceeding fine."

Finally, after such prolonged, intense, and sincere confession, Daniel makes a brief but earnest petition. But before
he does, the prophet reminds God that He had once delivered His people out of Egypt (v. 15), that His people
the Jews and Jerusalem the Holy City are now a cause
for reproach among nearby nations (v. 16), and that He is
known as a God of mercy (v. 18).

The petition itself is expressed with great intensity of feeling, the verbs falling like blows of a hammer (v. 19):

"O Lord, hear" this prayer and especially the petition about to be expressed.

"O Lord, forgive" the sin of the people in exile.

"O Lord, hearken and do," that is, give heed to the pressing need of the Jews and take action to deliver them.

"Defer not" to bring to an end the seventy-year captivity, in keeping with Jeremiah's prophecy.

It is in this petition that Daniel centers his hopes. The seventy years are all but completed, and the prophet longs for the fulfillment of God's gracious promises to Israel regarding His city and His people. "Defer not!" But defer God would. For though a small remnant would soon return to the land, the glorious restoration of the kingdom age, foretold in such prophecies as that of Amos (9:11–15), must wait. How long? The answer to that question is found in the crucial prophecy that now follows.

THE ANSWER TO THE PRAYER (9:20–27)

Does God answer prayer? He does, indeed, though not always as quickly and dramatically as in this instance. Daniel was still praying when Gabriel, the chief angel of divine communication, reached his side with an answer. Gabriel gave Daniel (and gives us) some interesting insights on what was happening in heaven while the prophet was praying on earth. First, it is obvious that God heard Daniel's prayer. He then responded to it by assigning to Gabriel the important mission of returning to earth (8:16) to bring important information to Daniel, the man "greatly beloved" of God. Judging from the length of Daniel's recorded prayer and the fact that Gabriel arrived before he finished, that trip took less than three minutes!

Says A. C. Gaebelein, "Heaven is not far away. There is no space and distance for God. What an encouragement to prayer this ought to be to God's people. The moment we pray in the Spirit and in His name our voices are heard in the highest heaven" (*The Prophet Daniel* [Grand Rapids: Kregel Publications, 1955], p. 129). Gabriel came from heaven to earth, from God's throne to Daniel's side, to give the prophet insight and understanding (v. 22). The message he brought to thus enlighten Daniel is found in the concluding four verses of chapter 9, and is clearly one of the most important prophecies of Scripture.

Certain facts must be established as basic and foundational to the understanding of this passage:

1. The prophecy concerns the Jews and Jerusalem (v. 24). In contrast to the prophecies of chapters 2 and 7, which related to the Gentile nations, this prophecy portrays only God's program for Israel. The church is not in view in any of these verses.

2. The scope of the prophecy covers not 70 years, as Daniel may have hoped, but 70 sevens of years. When Gabriel stated that seventy weeks were decreed concerning Jerusalem and the Jews, he meant that that would be the length of time in which God would fulfill all of His purposes regarding the nation of Israel. The word for "week" is literally "sevens" or *hepstads*. And, since ancient times, it has been generally agreed that the "weeks" or "sevens" were not weeks of days but weeks of years. Nothing else fits the context, for it is manifestly impossible to fit the events of 9:24–27 into 490 days or even weeks. The angel is thus saying to Daniel that 70 weeks of years, or a period of 490 years, is required to fulfill Israel's prophetic program.

3. This prophecy, it must be noted, concerns three deliverances. Daniel was greatly burdened about an early de-

liverance of the Jews from Babylon to return to Jerusalem. God was also interested in their deliverance from bondage to sin (at Christ's first Advent) and in the final deliverance of the Jews from oppression (at Christ's Second Coming). (Wood, *A Commentary on Daniel,* p. 244).

The angel Gabriel first summarized what was to transpire in seventy weeks of years by listing six important purposes of God's relating to the people of Israel and the Holy City, Jerusalem (v. 24).

1. "To finish the transgression"; that is, to restrain the great transgression or apostasy of Israel that brought such deep affliction.

2. "To make an end of sins"; that is, to put an end to the daily sins of God's people.

3. "To make reconciliation for iniquity"; that is, to provide atonement for sin.

4. "To bring in everlasting righteousness"; that is, to bring in a kingdom in which everlasting righteousness will prevail.

5. "To seal up the vision and prophecy"; that is, to bring to completion by fulfillment all prophecies of Scripture.

6. "To anoint the most holy"; that is, to anoint to religious service the most holy place of a yet future temple.

Sin was to be restrained and put to an end by atonement. Only the death of Christ could and did provide for these things. But an age in which there is everlasting righteousness, the fulfillment of all prophecy, and the presence of a restored temple must be future. History knows no such age. This age coincides with what the Scriptures elsewhere predict about conditions that will prevail when Christ returns.

We must conclude, therefore, that while the 70 weeks have begun, they have not yet been concluded. Thus, Gabriel's interpretation sketches the future of the nation of Israel and their city Jerusalem for the 490 years, or 70 weeks. But Gabriel has already learned that Daniel would not be satisfied with summaries and sketches and proceeds to show how the six divine purposes would be carried out. It seems that he anticipates the questions Daniel would naturally ask.

When will the "70 weeks" begin? The answer: not for almost 100 years! It is clearly stated (v. 25) that the beginning of this prophetic calendar will occur when a decree is issued "to restore and to build Jerusalem." Though several decrees were issued relative to the Jewish restoration, only one seems to deal directly with the rebuilding of Jerusalem, and that is the decree of Artaxerxes in 444 B.C. (Neh. 2:1–8). This must be the point of beginning for the 70 weeks, some 94 years from the time Daniel received this vision (538 B.C.).

How are the 70 weeks of prophetic history of the Jews divided up? Gabriel explains that the 70 weeks are divided into three sections or periods: (1) seven weeks of years (49 years); (2) 62 weeks of years (434 years), and (3) finally, one week of years (7 years).

What are the events that transpire in each period? During the first period—49 years (seven weeks)—the city of Jerusalem would be rebuilt (v. 25). While it is true that the walls of the city were repaired in 52 days under Nehemiah's leadership (Neh. 6:15), it apparently took much longer to clear out all of the debris and restore all of the damage inflicted on the city by Nebuchadnezzar. The point should not be lost, however, that Daniel's prayer would be answered; the Jews would be restored to their homeland, and eventually the city of Jerusalem would be rebuilt to her former state.

The second period—434 years (62 weeks)—sweeps on to "Messiah the Prince" (v. 25). While no predictions are found here concerning events in this period of time, prophecies of great struggles between nations inflicting suffering upon the Jews are given in Daniel's next and last vision (11:3–34). Here it is the termination of the 69th week (7 + 62) that is emphasized because that brings us to Christ—not, however, to His birth but apparently to the day He presented Himself to the nation as their Messiah-Prince. He did this only once in an official manner, at the time of the triumphal entry into Jerusalem (Matt. 21:1–11 and Zech. 9:9). Dr. Harold Hoehner convincingly demonstrated that it is precisely 483 years (49 + 434), using the Jewish calendar of 360 days, from the decree to rebuild Jerusalem in 444 B.C. to Christ's triumphal entry in A.D. 33 (*Bibliotheca Sacra*, January-March, 1975, pp. 62–64).

What happens after the 69th week? The question is answered in verse 26. It should be noted that a gap is now introduced between the 69th and 70th weeks because several very significant events are predicted to transpire after the 62 weeks (following the first seven, making a total of 69) but not during the 70th week.

1. Messiah will be cut off (v. 26). Messiah the Prince, it was announced, would be "cut off and have nothing" (literal). When Christ was crucified, He had nothing—He was deserted by friends and disciples, mocked by His enemies, and even forsaken by the Father. Yet, as Isaiah had so clearly prophesied, He was dying for the sins of others, dying to provide deliverance from bondage to sin, a deliverance so essential for the Jews and for all men (v. 24).

2. The city and sanctuary will be destroyed (v. 26). Though Jerusalem and its temple were to be rebuilt in the time of Ezra and Nehemiah, both would again be destroyed after the crucifixion of Christ. History records that Titus

Vespasian led four Roman legions to besiege and destroy Jerusalem in A.D. 70. Thus, the "people of the prince that shall come" are identified as Romans. The identity of the Roman prince will be discussed in the next verse.

Interestingly, General Titus ordered his soldiers to leave the temple intact, but Jesus had predicted to His disciples that "there shall not be left here one stone upon another, that shall not be thrown down" (Matt. 24:2). It is said that when a Roman soldier, on impulse, threw a flaming torch through an archway of the temple, the rich tapestries caught fire. The building soon became a raging inferno; the decorative gold melted and ran down into the cracks of the stone floors. When the remains cooled, the soldiers in their greed for wealth literally overturned the stones in search of the gold. The prophecy of Christ was grimly fulfilled.

3. War and desolation will be the continuing experience of the people of Israel (v. 26). While it is true that this part of the verse may refer only to the destruction of Jerusalem in A.D. 70, it seems to mean that the same terrible conditions will be characteristic of this age between the 69th and 70th weeks, coming to a consummation with the judgment of Israel's enemies at the Second Advent. Any study of the history of the Jews since the first century gives credence to this interpretation.

Leopold Cohn, a European rabbi, studied the prophecy of the 70 weeks and came to the conclusion, based on verse 26, that Messiah had already come because His coming was to be before the destruction had taken place in A.D. 70! Approaching an older rabbi, he asked where Messiah was. The rabbi said, "Go to New York and you will find Messiah there." Selling most of his belongings to buy passage to America, Mr. Cohn came to this country and wandered the streets of New York City, looking for Messiah. One day he heard singing coming from a building and went in, only to hear a clear gospel message. That night he received the Lord Jesus Christ as Messiah and Savior. Shortly after, Mr. Cohn bought a stable, swept it out, set up some chairs, and began to hold gospel meetings, the first outreach of what was to become the American Board of Missions to the Jews.

But what about the 70th week of this prophecy? If we follow the principle of literal interpretation, we must conclude that the final week of years is still future, because the phenomena described in verse 27 have simply not yet occurred. Furthermore, Jesus said (Matt. 24:15) that when the abomination of desolation appeared in the temple, it would mean the onset of the Great Tribulation, which is to be immediately followed by the Second Advent of Christ. Likewise, the person described in Daniel 9:27 is clearly the same as the wicked individual of Daniel 7:25 and Revelation 12 and 13, and that person is judged at Christ's Second Coming (Rev. 19:20). The day is coming, therefore, when God's prophetic program for Israel will be resumed. This will be signaled by the signing of a seven-year covenant with the restored Jewish nation by a certain person (Dan. 9:27). This person can be identified as a prince of the people who destroyed the city and the sanctuary, that is, a Roman prince. He is none other than Antichrist, the "little horn" of Daniel 7, the eventual head of the revived Roman empire of the Tribulation period.

A peace settlement in the Middle East? This is what Antichrist is powerful enough to negotiate, probably providing for an end to the Arab-Israeli controversy, guaranteeing Israel's security as a nation, and above all, giving the Jews access to the temple site so that a temple can be rebuilt and their ancient worship can be reestablished. Orthodox Jewish rabbis teach that the temple cannot be rebuilt till Messiah comes and that He will then initiate that project. Because Antichrist makes possible the rebuilding of a temple, many Jews will be deceived into thinking he is Messiah and will worship him.

But the protector of the Jews will become the great persecutor of the Jews. For after three and one-half years (Dan. 9:27), he will stop the sacrifices at the temple, desecrate the structure by erecting an image of himself in the Holy Place, and demand that he be worshiped as God (2 Thess. 2:4; Rev. 13:14). Those who do not comply will be subject to fierce persecution. Jesus foresaw this and warned, "When ye therefore shall see the abomination of desolation, spoken of by Daniel the prophet . . . then let them which be in Judaea flee to the mountains" (Matt. 24:15–16). Thus, what Antiochus Epiphanes, the Syrian ruler, did in the second century B.C. (Dan. 8:9–12), Antichrist will do in the end times.

Antichrist's evil and murderous reign will continue for the last half of the 70th week (three and one-half years). Then will come the "consummation" (9:27), with the coming of One more powerful than Antichrist, One who will cast this vile ruler into the lake of fire and destroy his army (Zech. 14:1–4; Rev. 19:11, 20–21). At last the nation of Israel will be delivered from her oppressors.

To summarize, the prophecy of the 70 weeks covers the history of Israel from the time of the rebuilding of Jerusalem in 444 B.C. to the Second Coming of Christ. During the first period of seven weeks (49 years), Jerusalem is restored. Toward the end of the second period of 62 weeks (434 years), Messiah appears and presents Himself officially to the nation. Following this, and between the 69th and 70th weeks, Messiah is cut off, Jerusalem is destroyed, and the age is marked as one of wars and desolations. The final period of one week (7 years) is dominated by the appearance of Antichrist who becomes Israel's protector and then persecutor till he is stopped by Christ on His return to earth.

Two Christians, observing the model of first-century Jerusalem at the Holy Land Hotel in that city, were discussing in particular the future rebuilding of the temple. A stranger stood nearby listening to their conversation and then introduced himself as a New York rabbi. He asked in amazement, "Do Christians really believe in the rebuilding of a temple in Jerusalem?"

"Haven't you read your prophets, Ezekiel and Daniel?" one of the Christians replied.

"No," the rabbi admitted, "because when I was studying to be a rabbi I was told not to read Daniel and was particularly forbidden to compute the prophecy of the seventy weeks in Daniel, chapter 9!"

The reason for such a prohibition? Because the prophetic books, especially Daniel 9, show that Messiah has already come.

An ancient rabbi said, "Let the bones of those who reckon the times tremble." Rather may it be said, "Let the hearts of those who reckon the times rejoice!" For Messiah has come and has provided salvation for all who believe.

"He came unto His own, and His own received Him not. But as many as received Him, to them gave He power to become the sons of God, even to them that believe on His name" (John 1:11–12).

DANIEL'S SEVENTY WEEKS

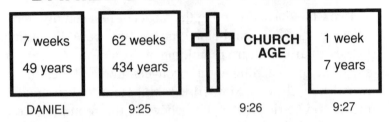

7 weeks	62 weeks		CHURCH AGE	1 week
49 years	434 years			7 years
DANIEL	9:25		9:26	9:27

9—THINK IT OVER

Often called "the backbone of prophecy," this chapter is rich with meaning—both personal and prophetic. It seems no coincidence that two-thirds of this passage deals with Daniel's intercessory prayer for his people, while only a few verses reveal the timetable for the events of the end of human history. This great chapter is more than a glimpse into the future—it is a call to repentance and prayer!

1. What earlier biblical prophecies led Daniel to prayer? What was his attitude in approaching God? (See Dan. 9:2–3; Jer. 25:11–12; 29:10.)

2. Does Daniel's prayer include praise? How essential is this element? (A majority of the Psalms exemplify the perfect balance of the elements of prayer that is pleasing to God.)

3. What do we learn from Daniel's uncompromising confession of sin? (See 9:14–15; 20–21.)

4. What does God's response to Daniel's prayer reveal? (See vv. 20–23.) How might this truth be applied to contemporary prayer requests?

5. Certain attitudes and sin may hinder prayer. Search for them in James 1:6–7; 4:3; 1 Peter 3:7; Matt. 6:5–6, 21–22; Ps. 66:18; Prov. 28:9; Isa. 59:2.

6. Though Daniel obviously did not pray "in Jesus' name," what benefit do modern-day believers enjoy? (See John 14:13–14; 15:16; 16:23, 26.)

7. What, specifically, does the Bible indicate we should pray about? (See 1 Tim. 2:1–2; Eph. 1:15–19; 3:14–19; 6:19.)

8. Outline the three periods of Daniel's seventy weeks. What events transpire in each period? (See vv. 25–27.)

9. What part of Israel's history is covered by the "seventy weeks"?

10. What person, prefigured by Antiochus Epiphanes, will dominate the final "week" of seven years? Describe his destiny. (See 9:27; Zech. 14:1–4; Rev. 19:11, 20–21.)

Daniel, in his careful preparation for approaching God, his praise of God's majesty, his uncompromising confession of sin, a fervor born of the burden he carried for his people, and his persistent supplication, illustrates the kind of prayer that God delights to answer. The prospect of soon seeing our Lord face to face should drive all believers to our knees in penitence and praise!

10

World History Unmasked

According to the *Canadian Army Journal,* a conscientious study of history has revealed the following figures concerning man's evil, warlike nature: "Since 3600 B.C. the world has known only 292 years of peace. During this period there have been 14,531 wars, large and small, in which 3 billion 640 million people have been killed. The value of the destruction would pay for a golden belt around the world about 100 miles wide and 33 feet thick! Since 650 B.C. there have been 1,656 arms races, only 16 of which have not ended in war! The remainder have terminated in the economic collapse of the countries concerned."

Since the world cast out the "Prince of Peace" the Lord Jesus Christ, by crucifying Him almost 2,000 years ago, there has not been one year without a war. In fact, in the last 500 years England has engaged in 78 wars; France, 71 wars; the Netherlands, 23; Spain, 64; Australia, 52; Germany, 23; Italy, 25; China, 11; Denmark, 20; Sweden, 26; Poland, 30; Russia, 61; Turkey, 43, and Japan, 9. European nations alone engaged in 74 wars during the lifetime of the first generation born in the twentieth century. Even America in its short history has engaged in 13 wars. And so, "man's inhumanity to man" continues. (*Our Daily Bread,* February, 1962).

How can we explain the fact that seemingly peaceful nations and intelligent people have been consistently driven to violence and collective murder almost since time began? The answer is found in this chapter of the prophecy of Daniel. In addition to the fact that man has an evil nature, there are demonic forces that are constantly active, working through leaders of human governments. The results are observable in the records of the past and the events of the present.

H. C. Leupold states, "We get a rare glimpse behind the scene of world history. There are spiritual forces at work that are far in excess of what men who disregard revelation would suppose. They struggle behind the struggles that are written on the pages of history" (*Exposition of Daniel,* pp. 457–58).

The remaining three chapters of Daniel form a unit. They contain the last of the prophet's four visions and describe the last recorded event in the aged prophet's life. As would be expected, these chapters embrace a climactic prophecy, one that builds on all that has been revealed before. A panorama of prophecy of Gentile times is given in chapter 2, and it is reviewed from another point of view in chapter 7, which expands the treatment of the final form of the fourth kingdom in the end times. Israel is the focus of chapter 8, and details are given about how that nation would fare under the second and third kingdoms, Medo-Persia and Greece. God's prophetic program for the Jews is outlined in chapter 9. Many more details are furnished in chapters 10–12 concerning the fate of the Jews in both the 69 weeks leading to the time of Messiah and in the 70th week, the time of Tribulation.

Chapter 10 is a prologue to chapters 11 and 12; it contains vital information that enables us to see behind the scenes of the conflicts affecting the nation of Israel.

THE REVELATION OF THINGS TO COME (10:1–3)

Daniel's final vision came in the year 536 B.C., when he was about 85 years old. How long and faithfully he had served God in a foreign land under a succession of mighty rulers! He had recently witnessed the answer to his prayer that God would restore the Jews to their homeland of Judah (Dan. 9). A remnant had returned under Zerubbabel as the decree of Cyrus allowed (Ezra 1:1), but the prophet had remained in Persia where he continued to serve God and his own people, the Jews.

The vision Daniel now received was of "a great conflict" (v. 1 NASB). This conflict would bring great suffering to the Jews, and Daniel grasped its significance. The explanation of the conflict is given in great detail in chapter 11 by an angelic messenger.

At the time Daniel received this disturbing revelation, he was mourning and fasting (vv. 2–3). Though the purpose for this is not explicitly stated, it may be safely assumed that Daniel was concerned about the welfare of the remnant that had gone back to rebuild the temple. And now that he had had a vision of a period of warfare, a time of intense hardship to come for his people, "he continued in mourning" (literal), perhaps praying for further light on the vision that implied a tragic future for the Jews.

Not many spiritual leaders have been so spiritually sensitive and burdened for the Lord's people as the prophet Daniel.

An outstanding example, however, of spiritual concern in more recent times was the late Dr. Andrew Bonar. After his death, his daughter led a Welsh evangelist into her father's church in Glasgow, Scotland. She pointed out a pew in the rear where, as a small girl, she had been asked to sit while her father went on into the empty sanctuary. After a long wait she stood up to look for him. He was seated in a pew, his head bent forward. Soon he moved to another pew, then another, and another. Sometimes she would see him carefully examine the nameplates to find the pews he desired. When she grew older she understood what her father had been doing on that day—he had been praying for his parishioners in the very spot where each worshiped. Such was the burden of Daniel for his people.

THE REVELATION OF GOD (10:4–9)

On the 24th day of the month Nisan, after the three weeks of fasting and prayer were concluded, Daniel was standing by the side of the river Tigris, no doubt having gone there on official business. He was probably meditating on the matter previously revealed to him (v. 1) when he suddenly saw a glorious vision of a "man clothed in linen" (v. 5). The man was dressed in garments normally worn by priests. His face and eyes flashed with brilliance, and his voice resounded with great force and power (v. 6). It was an awesome vision of overwhelming beauty, strength, and heavenly glory.

But who was this person? While some feel he was an angel, there is strong evidence to support the conclusion that He was the preincarnate Christ. The similarity, for example, between Daniel's vision here and John's vision of the glorified Christ (Rev. 1:12–20) is remarkable. And later in this expanded vision angels appeal to this "man clothed in linen" as having superior knowledge (12:6).

This then is the climactic spiritual experience in the life of Daniel, the man of God. At first he interpreted the dreams and visions of others (chaps. 2, 4, 5). Then he himself began to receive visions (chaps. 7, 8), being transported from one geographical area to another. Next, the angel Gabriel came to Daniel's side to give him insight and understanding regarding the future of his nation (chap. 9). Finally, the prophet is blessed with a glorious vision of the Son of God Himself.

In the light of the expanded revelation regarding the dark future of the nation of Israel soon to be brought to Daniel, it was appropriate that he first have a vision of the Lord to be reminded of His glory and sovereignty over men and nations.

The effect of this vision was overwhelming (vv. 7–9). The men with Daniel, though they did not see the Lord, sensed that something supernatural was taking place and fled. Daniel was left alone in the presence of the Lord and utterly collapsed, falling on his face in a deep swoon (Rev. 1:17).

Some might wonder at the fact that such a godly man as Daniel should find this vision of deity so overpowering and almost more than he could bear. But it speaks emphatically to us of the frailty of man in the presence of a holy God and of the fact that before Him all men must acknowledge their unworthiness.

Near the entrance to a large hospital in the eastern United States there stands a white marble statue of Christ. On its base are engraved the words, "Come unto Me, all ye that labor and are heavy laden, and I will give you rest." One day a cynical man walked around the statue, viewing it disapprovingly from every angle. A small girl stood and watched him for a time and then rushed up to him. "Oh, sir, you cannot see Him that way," she said. "You must get very close and fall upon your knees and look up."

The day is coming when all men will bow before Him and acknowledge that He is Lord (Phil. 2:10–11).

THE REVELATION FROM THE ANGELIC MESSENGER (10:10–21)

Angelic ministry to Daniel (vv. 10–11). While in a state of emotional shock, Daniel was touched by the hand of an angel. Since the previous vision was of the Son of God, it was probably Gabriel who now appeared to minister to the prophet. Daniel was brought back to consciousness by the angel's touch and enabled to rise to his knees. Then the angel spoke, exhorting him to stand erect and give careful attention to his words.

Angelic explanation to Daniel (vv. 12–14). The angel made it clear to Daniel that he had no reason to fear, for God had heard him from the very beginning of his period of fasting and praying and had dispatched a messenger in response. But why then was Daniel forced to wait for over three weeks?

The explanation is astonishing: a hostile spiritual power was able to intercept and delay the answer to Daniel's prayer for twenty-one days. The angel declared, "But the prince of the kingdom of Persia withstood me one and twenty days: but lo, Michael, one of the chief princes, came to help me; and I remained there with the kings of Persia" (v. 13).

A number of things are of compelling interest regarding this "prince of the kingdom of Persia." First, it is obvious that he was not a man, for no human being could have resisted a messenger from God. Second, since he did oppose God's emissary, he must have been one of Satan's evil messengers or demons. Third, his particular mission apparently was to influence the king of Persia against the people of God. Fourth, the angelic messenger, with the help of the chief angel Michael, was able to wrest the position of influence with the Persian king away from the evil angel before coming on to Daniel. Thereafter, he was able to influence the Persian rulers in favor of God's people, the Jews.

The angelic messenger then explained the purpose of his coming, namely, to describe what would happen to Israel in the "latter days" (v. 14). The prophecies of chapters 11 and 12 define these "latter days" to be the history of Israel in the "70 weeks" of her prophetic program with particular emphasis on her sufferings under Antiochus Epiphanes and his antitype—Antichrist of the end times.

Further angelic ministry to Daniel (vv. 15–19). Again Daniel was overcome with emotion, turning his face to the ground and remaining speechless. An angel touched the prophet's lips enabling him to speak, and Daniel responded by confessing that he simply felt unable to talk about these profound matters affecting his people. Touched once more by the angel (v. 18) and exhorted by him to be fearless and strong, Daniel then acknowledged that his strength had returned and he was ready for the angel to proceed with the important revelation concerning what would happen to his people in the "latter days" (v. 14).

Further angelic explanation to Daniel (vv. 20–21). The angel proceeded to explain more fully that the reason for his coming was not only in response to Daniel's prayers but also to engage in warfare with the previously mentioned evil supernatural powers. In fact, once he had completed imparting the information contained in chapters 11 and 12, the angel would return to the conflict with the demons to maintain his place of influence with the Persian kings and subsequently with the Grecian rulers. In this conflict the angel made clear that he fought alone except when he called on Michael for assistance.

But of chief interest were the matters about to be revealed, matters found recorded in the "writing of truth" (literal). Certainly the omniscient God has documented, long before they occur, the events that come to pass on earth. What is to follow then in chapters 11 and 12 is practically an abstract from the divine record and, as such, we are absolutely assured that it is "truth."

What an amazing, though mysterious chapter this is! From it we learn specifically that, while evil angels were seeking Israel's destruction, Gabriel, Michael, and the other angels of God were protecting their interests. But Daniel was to understand, and so are we, that this same struggle continues throughout all of world history. One wonders, in fact, what sort of conflict may be going on in the spiritual realm in our own precarious times.

This chapter gives us a glimpse into the unseen. It enables us to see that, behind the political and social conditions of the world in every generation, there has been angelic influence, both good and evil.

Of particular importance is the inside look at Satan's network of evil, for Satan and his evil spirits form a vast, invisible structure working behind the scenes in the governments of the world. Of course, on the other hand, the Holy Spirit as well as good angels minister through godly rulers (Heb. 1:14). But Satan and his demons are very active and seek to promote in every way possible the satanic world system.

Three times Jesus referred to Satan as "the prince of this world" (John 12:31; 14:30; 16:11). It was not a false claim that the devil made when he tempted Christ, showing Him all the kingdoms of the world and then saying to Him: "To

Thee will I give all this authority, and the glory of them; for it hath been delivered unto me; and to whomsoever I will I give it" (Luke 4:6). And so as Satan pleases, he assigns the control of the kingdoms of the earth to his own evil angels. Paul, in describing the hierarchy of evil beings in Satan's kingdom, refers to the "world-forces of this darkness" (Eph. 6:12 NASB). These are the evil spirits who rule in and through human rulers.

One scholar has written,

> History, since the fall of man, has been an unbroken attestation of the ominous fact of evil powers working in human rulers, whether it be a Pharaoh of Egypt, oppressing the people of God, or a Nebuchadnezzar, leading them into captivity, or a Nero, brutally torturing and massacring them. However, perhaps the most solemn demonstration of the utter barbarity and horrible cruelty and wickedness of men energized by demon power has, it seems, been reserved for the boasted civilization and enlightenment of the twentieth century. Hitler, the demon-energized and demon-directed scourge of Europe, has come and gone, leaving behind him only a trail of agonized suffering and state of chaos upon which atheistic communism is determined to perpetrate even greater evils. This system proclaims more blatant doctrines of demons, enslaves more persons, and murders even greater numbers of innocent victims. (Merrill F. Unger, *Biblical Demonology* [Wheaton, Ill.: Van Kampen Press, 1952], p. 197).

But the worst is yet to come. The Tribulation period will be a time of unprecedented demon activity. These emissaries of Satan will ultimately arouse the rulers of the world to assemble in a foolhardy and futile attempt to prevent the return of Christ and the establishment of His kingdom on earth (Rev. 19:19–20).

There is, of course, a personal application to all of this. Not only do Satan and his demons oppose God's purpose in the world, but they are also actively seeking to thwart the outworking of God's purpose in the lives of His children. Paul warned us, "Put on the full armor of God so that you can take your stand against the devil's schemes. For our struggle is not against flesh and blood, but against the rulers, against the authorities, against the spiritual forces of evil in the heavenly realms" (Eph. 6:11–12 NIV).

Robinson Crusoe taught his man Friday the doctrines of the Christian faith. When he came to the subject of the devil, he told Friday that he was God's enemy trying to defeat His purposes in the world. Friday asked, "Is God not as strong as devil?" Crusoe assured him that God was stronger and that Christians prayed to Him for victory over the devil. "But why God no kill devil so make him no more do wicked?" asked Friday. Crusoe was stumped and pretended not to hear, hoping Friday would forget the question. But he didn't, and finally Crusoe answered, "Well, God will punish the devil in the end." Friday persisted, "But why God not kill devil now?"

This is a question that may perplex many of us, and the ultimate answer lies with God alone. For reasons all His own, God allows evil to flourish and the Evil One to continue. But the Bible teaches clearly that Satan was judged at the cross (John 16:11) and that his doom is sealed, his final destruction certain.

Meanwhile, it is reassuring for the Christian to remember: "Greater is He that is in you [the Holy Spirit], than he that is in the world [Satan]" (1 John 4:4). Are you appropriating this resource for victory over the enemy?

10—THINK IT OVER

In this section we explore the subject of angels and demons. Because the workings of Satan and his demonic emissaries are exposed herein, we ought to pray for God's protection against those spirit beings who will attempt to block His purposes!

1. List the truths revealed about angels and demons in chapter 10. A good Bible dictionary will supplement your understanding of the spirit world.

2. Who is the "man" Daniel saw in his vision? (See 10:5–6. Compare with Revelation 1:12–20.)

3. How did Daniel respond to this vision? (See 10:8.) Compare Isaiah's response to his vision of the Lord. (See Isa. 6:1–8.)

4. What is the origin of angels? (See Ezek. 28:13, 15; Matt. 22:30.) How are they organized? (See Jude 9; Dan. 10:13; Eph. 6:12; Col. 1:16.)

5. How did angels minister to Christ? (See Luke 1:26–33; 2:13–14; Matt. 2:13; 4:11; 26:53; 28:2; Luke 22:43.)

6. How do angels minister to believers? (See Heb. 1:14; Acts 12:7; 27:23–24; Luke 16:22.)

7. What is the origin of demons? (See Matt. 23:24.) Since Satan is "the prince of the demons," it is likely that they are angels who fell with him. (See Ezek. 28:11–18; Isa. 14:14; 1 Tim. 3:6.)

8. How do demons attempt to thwart the purposes of God? (See Dan. 10:10–14; Matt. 9:33; Luke 13:11, 16; 1 Tim. 4:1; Rev. 16:13–16.)

9. Are demons out of God's control? (See 1 Sam. 16:14; 2 Cor. 12:7.) What is their destiny? (See Matt. 25:41; Rev. 20:10.)

10. What spiritual defenses does the believer have against Satan and his demons? (See Eph. 6:11–18; Heb. 7:25; James 4:7; 1 Peter 5:8–9; 1 John 2:1; 4:4.)

In this chapter we have been given an inside look at Satan's network of evil contrasted with the angelic hosts of heaven. Together they form "a vast, invisible structure working behind the scenes in the governments of the world." As believers, our "struggle is not against flesh and blood, but against the rulers, against the authorities, against the spiritual forces of evil in the heavenly realms" (Eph. 6:11–12 NIV). As we put on "the full armor of God," we are promised ultimate victory!

11

The Worst Is Yet to Come

A professor in a theological seminary taught that the Book of Daniel was written during the Maccabean period (second century B.C.) and not by the historic Daniel who lived in the sixth century B.C. A student asked the teacher how he could say that when Christ Himself said that Daniel wrote the book (Matt. 24:16). The professor replied sharply, "I know more about the Book of Daniel than Jesus did!"

This is only a sample of the attacks of the critics on the integrity of the Book of Daniel. Nowhere has that attack been more frontal than in relation to chapter 11. The reason is obvious. In the first 35 verses there are at least 135 prophecies that have been literally fulfilled and can be corroborated by a study of the history of the period.

Porphyry, a third-century A.D. philosopher, was one of the first to take the position that the Book of Daniel was historical fiction, written by someone in Judea about 165 B.C. to encourage resistance against Antiochus Epiphanes. His conclusion was based on the presupposition that predictive prophecy was impossible and that since chapter 11 speaks so accurately of events in the intertestamental period it must be history and not prophecy.

Unfortunately, the views of Porphyry did not die with him. Rather, as R. K. Harrison states, "Objections to the historicity of Daniel were copied uncritically from book to book, and by the second decade of the twentieth century no scholar of general liberal background who wished to preserve his academic reputation desired to challenge the current critical trend" (*Introduction to the Old Testament*, p. 1111).

Of course, the question ultimately resolves itself to the issue of whether God, the divine Author of Scripture, can predict future events. Says John F. Walvoord, "The issue is a clear-cut question as to whether God is omniscient about the future. If He is, revelation may be just as detailed as God elects to make it; and detailed prophecy becomes no more difficult or incredible than broad predictions" (*Daniel*).

The prediction of the future in detail (chap. 11) is tied to the prophecy of the 70 weeks (chap. 9). Daniel 11:1–35 describes the fate of Israel in the first 69 weeks of her prophetic history and verses 36–45 tell us of Israel's sufferings under Antichrist in the 70th week.

We must also remember the great lesson (chap. 10) that behind all the prophetic details (chap. 11) there is an unseen struggle between good and evil angels, each seeking to influence the fate of God's people, the Jews.

The prophetic history of Israel among the nations is described in Daniel 11. It falls into four divisions: prophecies concerning Persia (vv. 1–2), prophecies concerning Greece (vv. 3–4), prophecies concerning Egypt and Syria (vv. 5–35), and prophecies concerning Antichrist (vv. 36–45).

PROPHECIES CONCERNING PERSIA (11:1–2)

Only two events in the long and glorious history of the ancient Persian Empire (539–331 B.C.) are mentioned. First, the angelic visitor stated that he strengthened Darius in his first year (that is, in the year Babylon was conquered and Persia came to power). Though the purpose of this angelic ministry is not stated, it may be assumed that as a direct result the decree was issued permitting the Jews to return to Judah (Ezra 1). Thus, the chapter opens with an illustration of the influence of God's angels on the history of His people.

The second event the angel described is future for Daniel, and, in fact, the prophetic message of the chapter begins at this point (v. 2). The focus is on Xerxes (486–465 B.C.), who gathered an army of more than two and one-half million men and invaded Greece. It was an ill-fated adventure, however, for Xerxes was defeated. The Greeks, though the victors, remembered the invasion for years to come and longed for revenge.

PROPHECIES CONCERNING GREECE (11:3–4)

The prophecy now moves forward to Alexander the Great of Greece (356–323 B.C.), who retaliated against Persia by conquering that vast empire (8:4–8; 20–22). But Alexander's life and career were cut short by death and his great kingdom was divided among four of his generals (v. 4). In future years this event would have dire results for the Jewish people.

PROPHECIES CONCERNING EGYPT AND SYRIA (11:5–35)

The angel spoke of only two of the four divisions of Alexander's empire and of the great warfare between them. The two divisions were: Syria, ruled by Seleucus, one of Alexander's generals, and his successors; and Egypt, ruled by Ptolemy, another of Alexander's generals, and his successors. It is important to observe that the warfare between these dynasties greatly affected the Jews because they were between the anvil and the hammer.

It should be kept in mind that the detailed prophetic record is not without purpose. The earlier kings are described to provide a background for Antiochus Epiphanes (175–164 B.C.), and he is given ample attention because he foreshadows Antichrist of the end times. The movement of the chapter is toward these two significant personages who dramatically affect the fate of the Jews.

The prophecies regarding Egypt and Syria climaxing in Antiochus Epiphanes will be treated in five divisions.

Period one, 323–246 B.C. (vv. 5–6). First, two rival kings are introduced. They are the king of the south (Ptolemy I of Egypt) and one of his princes who outstripped him in power and became head of the Seleucid dynasty (Seleucus I of Syria). Some years later a diplomatic marriage was arranged between the two kingdoms.

The king of the south (Ptolemy Philadelphus) gave his daughter, Bernice, in marriage to the king of the north (Antiochus Theos), who was first forced to divorce his own wife, Laodice. After the death of Ptolemy, however, Antiochus took back his first wife who gained her revenge by murdering her husband, his Egyptian wife, and their infant son.

Period two, 246–240 B.C. (vv. 7–9). Ptolemy III, the brother of the murdered Bernice, now ruler in Egypt, invaded Syria and overran much of her territory. He also put the vindictive Laodice to death and returned to Egypt with great booty including, according to Jerome, 40,000 talents of silver and 2,500 images of gods previously taken out of Egypt to Persia by Cambyses. Seleucus II of Syria then attempted a revenge attack on Egypt but was forced to return to his own land without success (v. 9 NASB).

Period three, 223–187 B.C. (vv. 10–19). The angel now speaks in some detail of Antiochus III the Great and his struggles with the kings of Egypt. At first, Antiochus was highly successful, wresting control of Palestine from Egypt. Later, he was decisively defeated at Raphia on the southern Palestinian border by Ptolemy IV Philopater (vv. 11–12). Some years thereafter, allied with Philip V of Macedonia, Antiochus returned to wage war with Ptolemy V Epiphanes of Egypt. Antiochus was victorious, having also been aided by Jews who little realized what the Syrian victory would soon bring to their land and people (vv. 14–16). Egyptian rule over Palestine was thus brought to a final end. Syria would dominate from this time on.

Another diplomatic marriage was arranged between the two warring nations, Antiochus giving his daughter Cleopatra to be the wife of Ptolemy V in 192 B.C. (v. 17). Apparently Antiochus hoped his daughter would deliver Egypt into his control, but she remained loyal to her husband.

Still, Antiochus had not had enough of conquest. He next conquered many islands of the Aegean Sea and had early successes in Greece till he was defeated by the Roman army under Lucius Cornelius Scipio, also called Scipio Asiaticus. Returning in disgrace to his own land, Antiochus was killed while plundering a temple of its treasures (vv. 18–19).

Period four, 187–176 B.C. (v. 20). The son and successor of Antiochus the Great was Seleucus IV, who not only inherited a kingdom but also a great debt to Rome. Forced to pay 1,000 talents annually toward this debt, Seleucus sent tax collectors throughout his kingdom, including a man named

Heliodorus who plundered the temple in Jerusalem. Seleucus's reign was brief. He died mysteriously, perhaps poisoned by the treasurer of his kingdom.

Period five, 175–164 B.C. (vv. 21–35). The detailed history up to this point has provided a background for the debut of one of the two great personages of this chapter. He is Antiochus Epiphanes, the "little horn" (chap. 8), a "vile person" whose treatment of the Jewish people and religion in the intertestamental period foreshadows similar happenings in the Tribulation at the hands of the Antichrist. Antiochus Epiphanes's rise to power is described in verses 21–24. He seized the throne when it was not rightfully his and enjoyed some early military successes. He then deposed Onias III, the Jewish high priest (v. 22), and established his own priesthood. Forming leagues and breaking them, he extended his power throughout Syria, Palestine, Edom, Ammon, and Moab, using bribery to gain the support of the people (v. 24).

Antiochus's invasion and victory over Egypt are described in verses 25–28. With a firm base at home, Antiochus invaded Egypt, defeating Ptolemy Philometer in 170 B.C. on the border of Egypt. The treachery of Ptolemy's trusted courtiers is cited as a major reason for his defeat (v. 26). In working out truce arrangements, both kings also practiced treachery. The prophetic statement, "They shall speak lies at one table" (v. 27), seems all too characteristic of the peace conferences between men and nations, both ancient and modern. On his way back to Syria, Antiochus put down a small insurrection in Jerusalem and took the opportunity to plunder the temple (v. 28).

Antiochus's invasion and defeat in Egypt are described in verses 29–30. This second invasion of Egypt took place in 168 B.C., but as predicted, it was not successful. Met by

Romans near Alexandria, Antiochus was handed a letter from the Roman Senate ordering him not to fight against Egypt. When the Syrian king hesitated, the Roman consul drew a circle around Antiochus in the sand and told him he must make a decision before stepping out of the circle. Humiliated, frustrated, and enraged, Antiochus turned back toward Syria, having traveled the long distance to Egypt for nothing.

Antiochus's persecution of the Jews is described in verses 30–35 (see also 8:10–14). Again Antiochus stopped in Palestine en route to Syria, this time venting his frustration and anger against the Jews. Conspiring with apostate Jews, he stopped daily sacrifices at the temple and desecrated the sanctuary by erecting, in place of the brazen altar, a statue of the Greek god Zeus. This was the abomination that made the temple desolate, for no faithful Jew would think of approaching such an idol to worship Jehovah (v. 31).

During those awful days some, led and inspired by the Maccabees (v. 32), resisted heroically, but thousands of others were slaughtered (vv. 33–34). The suffering of the Jews under Antiochus Epiphanes, however, had a refining purpose and this refining or purging process is predicted to continue till the "time of the end" (v. 35). This key expression provides the transition from Antiochus Epiphanes to Antichrist, from the past to the future, from history to prophecy. As will be demonstrated, the tenor of this remarkable prophecy changes as the future persecution of Israel in the Tribulation period comes into view.

The approximately 135 specific prophecies in the first 35 verses of this chapter have been fulfilled with amazing accuracy, as would be expected of a divine revelation. There is every reason to believe, therefore, that the remaining prophecies of the chapter will have the same precise and literal fulfillment in the future.

Dr. E. Schuyler English once told of a man on Long Island who was able to satisfy a lifelong ambition by purchasing a very fine barometer. When he unpacked the instrument, he was dismayed to find that the needle appeared to be stuck, pointing to the section marked "Hurricane." After shaking the barometer vigorously, the man wrote a scorching letter to the store from which he had purchased the instrument and, on his way to his office in New York the next morning, mailed the protest. That evening he returned to Long Island to find not only the barometer missing, but his house also. The barometer's needle had been right—there was a hurricane!

PROPHECIES CONCERNING ANTICHRIST (11:36–45)

"What is past is prologue." The climax of this chapter is now reached, and it is clearly seen that the suffering of the Jews under Antiochus Epiphanes (175–164 B.C.) was a foreshadowing of their deeper afflictions under the sinister figure now described, the Antichrist. The tenor of the prophecy begins to change (v. 36). All intervening history is passed over, and there is a leap of centuries to the "time of the end" and to a renewed struggle between the king of the north and the king of the south.

Though not all have agreed, the evidence seems conclusive that the spotlight now falls on an evil ruler of the last days—Antichrist. (1) According to the angel's words, the scope of this prophecy was to include the "latter days" (10:14). (2) In the opening verses of this section (vv. 36–39), introductory statements are made as if this person is being introduced in this context for the first time. This corresponds with the fact that the story of Antiochus in relation to the Jews was brought to completion (v. 35). (3) The prophecies (through v. 35) find fulfillment in history, but there is no historical correspondence with what now follows. (4) This king is actually distinguished from the king of the north (v. 40). Therefore, he cannot be Antiochus Epiphanes. (5) The entire section (vv. 36–45) corresponds remarkably with other recognized prophecies of the final Antichrist (Dan. 7:24–27; 8:23–25; 9:26–27; 2 Thess. 2:4ff; Rev. 13, 17). (6) In connection with this person's rule there will occur the time of Great Tribulation (12:1).

The following letter to the editor appeared in *Time* magazine concerning a certain diplomatic figure of our time: "A man who does not make value judgments could be dangerous. A man who does not ask who is right may operate with a blank and pitiless conscience. If the same man happens to be amassing ever greater power and popularity, watch out, world! A brilliant mind, a passionate ego and an imagination unfettered by any moral absolutes concoct the ultimate delusion: Your savior has come—fall down and worship him" (April 22, 1974).

The Scriptures make it clear that such an ominous figure will appear on the world scene. His character, career, and fate are clearly described to Daniel by the angel who makes at least twelve declarations concerning him:

1. He will act in self-will (v. 36). One writer describes him as "a person who will represent the acme of human self-love, self-will, and self-exaltation—and, accordingly, the acme of insolence, impiety, and defiance toward God" (*Bible Knowledge,* June, 1968, p. 117).

2. He will exalt himself (v. 36). What a contrast with Jesus Christ who "emptied Himself, taking the form of a bond-servant, and being made in the likeness of men" (Phil. 2:7 NASB).

3. He will magnify himself above every god (v. 36). Like Lucifer who said, "I will be like the Most High" (Isa. 14:14), Antichrist will arrogantly assert his supremacy above all deities. Paul, writing of the man of sin, said, "Who opposeth and exalteth himself above all that is called God, or that is worshiped; so that he as God sitteth in the temple of God, shewing himself that he is God" (2 Thess. 2:4).

4. He will blaspheme the true God (v. 36). This is amplified in the Book of Revelation (13:6) where it is said of the Beast, "And he opened his mouth in blasphemy against God, to blaspheme His name, and His tabernacle, and them that dwell in heaven."

5. He will prosper for a limited period of time (v. 36). Even when Antichrist rules, God will control history and will permit this evil person to thrive for only a limited period of time (seven years, according to 9:27).

6. He will be an irreligious person (v. 37). Antichrist will completely disregard his religious heritage ("the gods of his fathers") and the messianic hope. The expression "desire of women" probably refers to the desire of Hebrew women in premessianic times to be the mother of the Messiah. It is plain then that Antichrist will reject any and all deities and specifically the Lord Jesus Christ.

7. He will place confidence in military might (vv. 38–39). In essence, he will worship the god of war and will expend all his financial resources to support military goals and activities. Launching attacks on other kingdoms, Antichrist will quickly conquer them and then reward with allotments of land those who give obeisance to him.

8. His military might will be challenged (v. 40). As background for the conflict now described, it must be remembered that Antichrist, as head of the revived Roman Empire, makes a covenant with Israel at the beginning of the Tribu-

lation (9:27), guaranteeing her borders. An alliance formed by the king of the south (probably Egypt and allies) and the king of the north (probably Russia) will challenge that protective treaty by a simultaneous invasion of the land of Israel "with chariots, and with horsemen, and with many ships." Will the invading armies actually use horses in a day of jet aircraft and nuclear weaponry? Probably the weapons listed are to be understood in terms of their modern counterparts. However, it is possible that societal upheavals in that day will be such as to affect the military industry and that, in part at least, armies will be forced to revert to the use of simpler weapons and means of conveyance.

9. He will be initially victorious in battle (vv. 40–43). Responding to Israel's cry for assistance, Antichrist and his forces will invade from the west and win an early victory over the kings of the north and south, probably near Megiddo. This will probably take place at the midpoint of the Tribulation period and mark the beginning of the campaign of Armageddon, a war that will rage for three and one-half years and reach its climax at Jerusalem (Zech. 14:2). Antichrist will quickly pursue the defeated Egyptian army to their land, where he will plunder the great treasures of that country. Libya and Ethiopia will also then be attacked and defeated.

10. He will face renewed conflict (v. 44). Reports will reach Antichrist in Africa that the king of the north has regrouped for another attack and that massive armies from the east are marching toward Palestine (see Rev. 9:13–21; 16:12). Antichrist will react quickly, counterattacking with great force and fury. The result? "And he will go forth with great wrath to destroy and annihilate many" (11:44 NASB).

11. He will establish headquarters in Jerusalem (v. 45). Having won another remarkable victory, Antichrist will

make Jerusalem his capital, a base from which to continue his persecution of the Jews. Upon entering the land (v. 41), Antichrist breaks covenant with the Jews. No longer their protector, he becomes their vicious persecutor. Now he will attempt to complete the evil work of exterminating the Jews, but is to be hindered by an invasion of armies from the north, south, and east. Jerusalem, Antichrist's capital, will be caught in the middle.

12. He will "come to his end" (v. 45). A startling thing will happen. The armies of the nations assembled to attack Jerusalem will look up, astonished to see Jesus Christ and His heavenly armies descending to earth (Zech. 14:1–4). According to John's vision of this great event, the armies of earth will turn from their conflict to attempt to prevent Christ's return. Needless to say, the attempt will be futile as those armies will be destroyed by the word of His mouth, and Antichrist will be cast alive into the lake of fire (Rev. 19:19–21).

We look up from the pages of Scripture, especially of this chapter, and see an alignment of nations and armies with reference to the little nation of Israel that make possible the early fulfillment of these prophecies.

We also observe what appears to be a growing interest in this evil world ruler of the end time, the Antichrist. The movie, *The Omen,* seen in theaters and on television, presents an imaginary account of how Antichrist will be introduced into the world. A *Time* magazine review of the movie stated, "The movie stretches a prophecy about the return of the Prince of Darkness, taken from *Revelations* [sic], to fit certain events of our time—the creation of Israel and the Common Market, of all things—then argues persuasively that if Satan were to return in disguise he would logically want to be a member of a rich political family so that he could position himself for maximum mischief making" (June 28, 1976).

The film was such a success at the box office that sequels were planned, with the leading character (Antichrist) pictured as a 12-year-old, a young man, and a western leader who guides his people to Armageddon.

We do not look for Antichrist, however, but for Jesus Christ. He is coming to take believers to be with Himself before these dark prophecies unfold on earth (John 14:1–3; 1 Thess. 4:13–18). The most important matter a person will ever face is that of his relationship to God's Son, who by His death at His first coming paid the penalty for sin. He now offers forgiveness of sin and eternal life. "For the wages of sin is death; but the gift of God is eternal life through Jesus Christ our Lord" (Rom. 6:23).

11—THINK IT OVER

"Prophecy is history pre-written." In God's omniscience, He has recorded for us many of the most profound prophecies in all of the Scriptures—both fulfilled and unfulfilled. Will we pass over them, missing their deepest significance, because of the difficulty of these passages, or will we lay aside our preconceived notions and open our hearts to the interpretation of the Holy Spirit?

1. Prayerfully read this chapter in several versions, including a paraphrase or modern English translation.

2. Ask yourself: Would God have preserved this detailed prophetic record had He not wanted us to study and understand it? Of what purpose is this prophecy? (See text, p. 163.)

3. In Daniel 11:1–35, 135 prophecies have been historically fulfilled. What can one thus conclude about the prophecies cited in 11:36–45?

4. In this chapter, when does past prophecy end and future prophecy begin? Verse 40 speaks of the time of the end. Could verses 36–39 be included? Have the events described in these verses taken place in history?

5. Outline the character (11:36–39) and activity (11:40–45) of the Antichrist. How does he relate to the nation of Israel?

6. What does the Book of Revelation reveal about the Antichrist? (See 13:1–18; 17:12–17; 19:19–20.)

7. How does the Antiochus of history (Dan. 11:21–35) relate to the Antichrist of prophecy (11:36–45)?

8. Daniel 11:36–45 basically describes events of the Tribulation—that seven-year period of God's wrath on unbelieving Jews and Gentiles. Read several passages from Scrip-

ture that speak of the Tribulation. (See. Jer. 30:7; Dan. 9:24–27; Matt. 24:4–18; Rev. 6–19.)

9. According to 1 Thessalonians 1:10, 5:9, 2 Thessalonians 2:1–10, and Revelation 3:10, are believers promised deliverance from this time of wrath?

10. How should a knowledge of the details of the Tribulation affect one's attitude toward evangelism?

Scripture reveals the way of salvation as well as the consequences of neglecting God's provision. In view of this powerful study on "the end times," believers can share the gospel and thus spare friends and neighbors the horrors of "the time of wrath."

12

All's Well That Ends Well

When a film entitled *I Am a Jerusalemite* was shown in Israel, a young man was asked to describe his feelings toward religion, particularly Orthodox Judaism and Christianity. Concerning Judaism, he said, "I am impressed because many of the things prophesied in the Old Testament seem to be coming to pass. And now they tell me the Mount of Olives will be divided in two! But," he continued, "Christianity makes me very uneasy." He paused, looking thoughtful. "There is something just around the corner. I can feel it—but I don't know what it is!"

In the final chapter of Daniel, continuing the thought of chapter 11, we are told what is around the corner for Israel— a time of deep trouble for some. For others, there is also hope.

THE TRIBULATION OF ISRAEL (12:1a)

At the time of the events described in 11:40–45 (the rule of the Antichrist), Michael, the special angelic protector of the nation of Israel, will "stand up." Revelation 12:7–9 records what Michael will do when he rises up: He and his angels will wage war in heaven against the dragon (Satan) and his angels. The battle will be final and decisive, with Satan and his host vanquished from heaven and cast down to the earth. But this victory will precipitate the Great Tribulation. Satan will vent his wrath against Israel, but a remnant will find refuge in the wilderness and there be sustained and protected for the last three and one-half years of the Tribulation (Rev. 12:12–14).

It is to this unprecedented time of trouble that the angelic messenger to Daniel now refers. A major theme of the Scriptures, the Tribulation is predicted in such passages as Deuteronomy 4:30, Jeremiah 30:7, and Joel 2:2 in the Old Testament. Likewise, in the New Testament, it is described in detail (Rev. 6–19) and referred to by Jesus Christ in language quite similar to that of Daniel 12:1. Jesus said, "For then shall be great tribulation such as was not since the beginning of the world to this time, no, nor ever shall be. And except these days should be shortened [that is, terminated by His return] there should no flesh be saved" (Matt. 24:21–22).

THE DELIVERANCE OF ISRAEL (12:1b)

David Baron once declared, "Just as that shepherd of Bethlehem slew both lion and bear and saved from their jaws the lamb which was taken possession of by them as their prey, so will the Shepherd of Israel save the remnant of His people, from the hands and jaws of those who are stronger than they; and slay them who devoured, broke in pieces and stamped with their feet His chosen, with a fierceness exceeding that of the bear and the lion."

Israel's time of trouble, which will affect all the world as well, is especially designed to prepare her for the coming of Messiah. In the closing days of the Tribulation, the surviving Jews will apparently search the Scriptures, seeking the reason for the bitter trials that have come upon them. They will discover that it is because of their rejection of Jesus Christ and they will then, many scholars believe, pour out their national confession in the moving words of Isaiah 53. Following this, they will plead for Messiah's return, perhaps in these words, "Oh that Thou wouldst rend the heavens, that Thou wouldst come down" (Isa. 64:1).

A Jew in a New York synagogue was once heard praying, "Oh that Thou wouldst rend the heavens, that Thou wouldst come down, Lord. . . . Send Messiah, and should Jesus of the Gentiles be the One, grant us a sign that we may be sure it is really so and forgive our guilt toward Him!"

In response to Israel's desperate prayer, Jesus Christ will come, bringing deliverance to His people. That deliverance will be both physical (Zech. 14:1–4) and spiritual (12:10–13:1). But even at the return of Christ, not every Jew will believe (Ezek. 20:33–38). The ones delivered in the fullest sense are those whose names "shall be found written in the book" (Dan. 12:1). This special company is composed of those who acknowledge Jesus Christ as Messiah and Savior.

The Reverend J. C. Hoover, at one time a missionary to the Jews in Denver, was riding in a car with a Jewish rabbi. As they drove up in front of the synagogue, the rabbi said, "Mr. Hoover, you Gentile Christians are looking for the Second Coming of your Savior, Jesus Christ, and we Jews are looking for the first coming of our Messiah. Who knows but what He might be the same person!" Then he paused before asking, "Mr. Hoover, how do you think we will recognize our Messiah?"

Quietly and prayerfully Mr. Hoover read the words of the prophet Zechariah, "And they shall look upon Me whom they have pierced."

The rabbi was silent as he got out of the car and walked slowly into his synagogue.

THE RESURRECTION OF ISRAEL (12:2)

Deliverance, both physical and spiritual, is promised to those believing Jews still alive at the close of the Tribulation. But what of the many godly Jews who die under the cruel persecution of the Antichrist? Will they miss the blessings of the kingdom reign of Christ?

We are now assured that there will be a resurrection of the righteous Israelites who died in this previous "time of trouble" described in the immediate context. This interpretation is enforced by Revelation 20:4–6, where martyred Tribulation saints are seen to be raised from the dead and exalted at the beginning of the millennial reign. It seems proper to believe that righteous Gentiles martyred in the Tribulation are raised at this time as well, as are all Old Testament saints. The righteous dead of the church age are raised at the beginning rather than at the end of the Tribulation (1 Thess. 4:16).

But our verse (12:2) refers also to the resurrection of the wicked ("some to everlasting life, and some to shame and everlasting contempt"). Does this mean, as some insist, that at the end of time there is to be but one general resurrection? As a matter of fact, a thousand years separate the two resurrections referred to here. This is made clear in Revelation 20:4–6, 12–15. After speaking of the resurrection of the righteous, John stated, "But the rest of the dead lived not again until the thousand years were finished" (Rev. 20:5).

THE REWARD OF ISRAEL (12:3)

Following the resurrection, righteous Israel will be rewarded. These faithful ones are described as being "wise" and their wisdom is illustrated by the fact that, during the Tribulation, believing Jews will influence many to turn from all that Antichrist stands for and to embrace faith in God and in His Son, Jesus Christ.

Their reward will be that they will shine with the same glory as the heavens and the stars. Thus, they will manifest the glory of God, as do the heavens (Ps. 19:1).

What a strong challenge for believers in this age to be faithful witnesses. Though wisdom is measured today according to other standards, the fact remains that in God's eyes, "He that winneth souls is wise" (Prov. 11:30).

It has been well said that if you want to plant something that will last a year, plant a flower; if you want to plant something that will last a lifetime, plant a tree; and if you want to plant something that will last forever, plant the good news of the gospel in the heart of a lost person.

CONCLUSION (12:4–13)

The angel's long message concerning Israel in the latter days (10: 14) has come to an end. Daniel is now instructed (v. 4) to preserve the angel's words, as well as the other portions of this book, "until the time of the end" or the Tribulation period. The prophecies of this book will certainly have primary application to those living in that period and will be of great comfort and help to the faithful, who will be enabled to understand God's purposes and program. The fact that we still have the Book of Daniel after 2,500 years is an indication that it is being preserved for the end times.

Then "many shall run to and fro, and knowledge shall be increased." On the basis of this verse, Isaac Newton predicted that the day would come when the volume of knowledge would be so increased that people would be able to travel 50 miles an hour! In response, Voltaire cast great ridicule upon Newton and the Bible.

This cryptic expression is best understood to mean that people in the Tribulation will run about seeking answers to questions about the climactic events of their times and that they will find those answers through increased knowledge of the Book of Daniel.

An increased knowledge of the Scriptures in our crisis times would also provide the answers we so desperately seek. Yet not long ago an English clergyman recommended that Bible reading be banned for a year! He said, "The present situation regarding the Scriptures is intolerable. They represent an intellectual incubus that cannot be removed until an almost completely new start is made with this most controversial document." Controversial document? Peter affirms, instead, that the Bible is "a light that shineth in a dark place" (2 Peter 1:19). To read and study it is to find comfort, help, and instruction in any age.

Two questions and their answers bring us to the conclusion of the book:

The angel's question and the reply (vv. 5–7). As Daniel stood alongside the Tigris River, he observed three persons, one on either side and one above the river. These are probably to be identified as two angels who were in communication with the Lord Himself, the Person described so gloriously before by the prophet (10:5–6). One angel inquired from the Lord as to how long it would be "to the end of these wonders" (v. 6b).

The answer makes it clear that the question concerned the time of oppression under the Antichrist. The Lord replied on solemn oath that those extraordinary events will last "a time, times, and a half," or three and one-half years (see 7:25; 9:27; 12:11–12; Rev. 11:2; 12:6, 14; 13:5). Dating from the time Antichrist will break his covenant with the Jews to begin his outrageous persecution of them, it will be three and one-half years till the consummation at the Second Advent.

Daniel's question and the reply (vv. 8–13). The prophet was still perplexed, and so he courageously asked the Lord, "What will be the outcome of these events?" (v. 8 NASB). The Lord gave a fourfold answer.

First, Daniel was assured that the shattering events previously described were far in the future (v. 9). Furthermore, in "the time of the end," oppressed Israel will understand these prophecies (see 12:4).

Second, the prophet was given a partial answer to his question regarding the outcome of the events of the Tribulation. The Lord explained that the sufferings of that future day will result in the spiritual cleansing of some but the hardening of others in their wickedness (v. 10).

Third, the Lord gave some further information regarding the chronology of the time of the end. He explained that there will be 1,290 days or three and one-half prophetic years plus thirty days from the middle of the Tribulation (see 9:27) to an undefined termination.

What will be the purpose for the additional thirty days beyond the Second Advent of Christ? Perhaps it will take this extra month for the judgment of the nations. This is described as an event to transpire just after the Lord's return (Matt. 25:31–46). In addition, the regathering and judgment of Israel, described in Ezekiel 20:34–38, must be accomplished. Both judgments are necessary to determine who will be worthy to enter the kingdom.

Further, the Lord pronounced a blessing on those who came to 1,335 days or three and one-half prophetic years plus seventy-five days. An additional forty-five days beyond the probable completion of the judgments will be required.

Leon Wood offers the following credible explanation: "It may be the time necessary for setting up the governmental machinery for carrying on the rule of Christ. The true and full border of Israel (from the River of Egypt to the Euphrates [Gen. 15:18]) will have to be established, and appointments made of those aiding in the government. A period of 45 days would again seem to be reasonable in which to accomplish those matters" (*A Commentary on Daniel*, pp. 328–29).

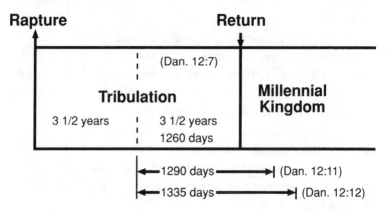

Adapted from a drawing appearing in Ezekiel / Daniel by Irving Jensen, (Moody Press, 1968. p. 92).

Finally, Daniel was told to go his way till the end of life would come and he would rest in death, later to be raised to share in the glory of Christ's millennial kingdom (v. 13).

Thus the book that reveals so much about God's plans for the nations of the world closes with the comforting revelation that He also has a plan for individuals. And that plan includes eternal life for those who believe.

"For God so loved the world, that He gave His only begotten Son, that whosoever believeth in Him should not perish but have everlasting life" (John 3:16).

12—THINK IT OVER

For all the dire predictions prophesied for the godless, the final chapter of the Book of Daniel promises deliverance, resurrection, and reward for the faithful. As one young Israeli observed, "There is something just around the corner. I can feel it . . ."

1. To what specific event does the "time of trouble" refer? (See 12:1.)

2. Who are those found written in the book? How will they be rescued? (See 12:1.)

3. What two kinds of resurrection are mentioned in 12:2?

4. How does John 5:28–29 contribute to Daniel's teaching concerning the resurrection?

5. When will the saints mentioned in 1 Thessalonians 4:16 be raised? Those of Revelation 20:4?

6. What does Revelation 20:5, 11–15 reveal about the resurrection of the unjust? When will that resurrection take place?

7. What is the condition of the dead in Christ between death and resurrection? (See 2 Cor. 5:1–8; Phil. 1:23.)

8. What chronology of events is revealed in Daniel 12:6–12?

9. How should the doctrine of the resurrection affect unbelievers?

10. What promise was made to Daniel concerning the resurrection? (See 12:13.)

An English clergyman recommended that the reading of the Bible be banned for one year. "The present situation regarding the Scriptures is intolerable," he said. "They represent an intellectual incubus that cannot be removed until an almost completely new start is made with this most controversial document." Believers, beware! We must learn how to stand against such heresy and affirm, with Peter, that the Bible is "a light that shineth in a dark place" (2 Peter 1:19). As the author states, "To read and study it is to find comfort, help and instruction in any age."

Note to the Reader

The author and publisher invite you to share your response to the message of this book by writing Discovery House Publishers, P.O. Box 3566, Grand Rapids, MI 49501 U.S.A.